Citizen Sensing for Risk Response

"In '*Citizen Sensing for Risk Response*', Anna Berti Suman provides a critical review of notions that are often contested nowadays, such as public and environmental health, and risk governance. She carefully engages with such concepts to identify gaps in existing literature and to develop a theory on how forms of spontaneous environmental monitoring from civil society could strengthen institutional risk governance. In doing so, she sheds light on an approach that can be very relevant for addressing and mediating conflicts stemming from societal management of complex risk problems. The book will appeal to a large societal audience, including environmental interest groups, non-governmental organizations, researchers, governmental authorities, and professionals in the sector including the profession that I represent, i.e., environmental lawyers."

—Veronica Dini *Environmental and Climate Lawyer, Co-Founder of Systasis, Centre for the Prevention and Management of Environmental Conflicts, Head of Dini-Saltalamacchia Law Firm, Milan, Italy*

"The contribution by Anna Berti Suman is going to be crucial in the field as civic initiatives such as the one I represent often feel unrepresented by the realm of research. With her volume, Berti Suman offers strategic knowledge at the intersection of environmental law inquiry, socio-legal research on field and risk governance studies. There is often a disconnect between (academic) research and small-scale citizen sensing activities. The book effectively bridges the gap between the perspective of local citizen sensing communities and overarching discourses on risk and risk governance."

—Giorgio Santoriello *Activist, Founder and president of the association Cova Contro for environmental civic monitoring in Basilicata, Italy*

Anna Berti Suman

Citizen Sensing for Risk Response

Exploring Contributions to Risk Governance

palgrave
macmillan

Anna Berti Suman
The University of Padua
Padua, Italy

Formely The European Commission
Joint Research Centre
Ispra, Italy

ISBN 978-3-032-03938-5 ISBN 978-3-032-03939-2 (eBook)
https://doi.org/10.1007/978-3-032-03939-2

This work was supported by Joint Research Centre, European Commission.

This Palgrave Macmillan imprint is published by the registered company Springer Nature Switzerland AG
The registered company address is: Gewerbestrasse 11, 6330 Cham, Switzerland

To Fabrizio, for his wise advice and tireless support

Preface

'Citizen sensing', entailing grassroots-driven monitoring initiatives based on sensor technology, is increasingly entering the debate on environmental risk governance. When lay people distrust official information or just want to fill data gaps, they may resort to sensors and data infrastructures to visualize, monitor and report risks caused by environmental factors to public health. Although through possible frictions with the institutions or with other stakeholders, citizen sensing may ultimately have the potential to contribute to institutional risk governance. Whereas studies on broader citizen science and on citizen sensing often focus on the learning gains for the participants, this book provides a novel insight into the field rather exploring the potential for the sensing citizens to concretely influence risk governance by filling (intentional or accidental) official informational gaps. Citizen sensing proves to be a practice having the potential to tackle institutional struggles in the way the data provided to the public over an (environmental) risk problem is gathered, disseminated and communicated. This essentially unveils the issue of a perceived legitimacy gap in current (environmental) risk governance. Nonetheless, it also opens avenues for a more inclusive and transparent governmental response to pressing and complex risks.

Dealing with a timely issue, that is, the key role of information in governing risks, as visible during the COVID-19 pandemic, the book offers a discussion relevant for academics, practitioners, policy-makers and academics. From a review of the existing academic and grey literature, it emerges that the perspective adopted in this book is unique. Indeed, the idea of combining the elements of risk, technology, the grassroots-drive and distrust to form a lens of analysis for citizen sensing practices has not been used to date. In spite of the existence of numerous studies bringing together technology and risk, as well as citizens and technology, and lastly citizens and (dis)trust, (dis)trust and technology, and (dis)trust and risk, it is instead hard to find the grassroots and distrust element clearly related to technology and risk and more specifically applied to citizen sensing (/citizen science/community-based monitoring etc.) Under this perspective, the lens of analysis embraced here not only operates as an effective selection criterion but also represents an element of novelty of the manuscript. Furthermore, the mixed-methods approach adopted to target the research aim, combining theoretical reflections with ethnography, can enrich the field.

The book demonstrates that citizen sensing has the potential to contribute to the achievement of a more accountable and inclusive risk governance, especially in case of highly debated, ambiguous and politicized risks. This may improve risk governance by means of a twofold process, i.e., an initial conflict stage (i.e., frictions of the citizen sensing initiative with appointed institutions) which may lead to convergence (that is, cooperation with the risk governors). It is argued that a clash of methods between the grassroots and the institutional risk governance is regarded as constructive and positive. When a later convergence with the institutional system occurs ('policy uptake'), I argue that this outcome should be regarded as a success for the initiative and for the institution and a demonstration that the two approaches can strengthen and complement each other. However, context-dependency and other nuances are outlined as important factors to be considered.

Anna Berti Suman
The University of Padua
Padua, Italy

Formely The European
Commission Joint Research
Centre
Ispra, Italy

Acknowledgements I would like to acknowledge my gratitude to the colleagues of the Tilburg Institute for Law, Technology, and Society (TILT), Tilburg Law School, Tilburg University (The Netherlands) and of the European Commission's Joint Research Centre, Digital Economy Unit, Ispra (Italy), for having inspired and guided this research. Furthermore, I wish to thank the interviewed experts from several institutions that took the time to answer my inquiries and followed over the time the evolution of this study. In addition, I am grateful to all the participants of this research, especially those from the cases mentioned. Lastly, I thank the anonymous reviewers that provided useful feedback to the shaping of this manuscript.

This study was developed also thanks to the support of the Marie Skłodowska-Curie Individual Fellowship, grant n. 891513, awarded to author Anna Berti Suman under H2020-EU (the "Sensing for Justice—SensJus" project). The open access publication has been ensured thanks to the funding of the European Commission's Joint Research Centre.

Competing Interests The author has no competing interests to declare that are relevant to the content of this manuscript.

Visual Summary

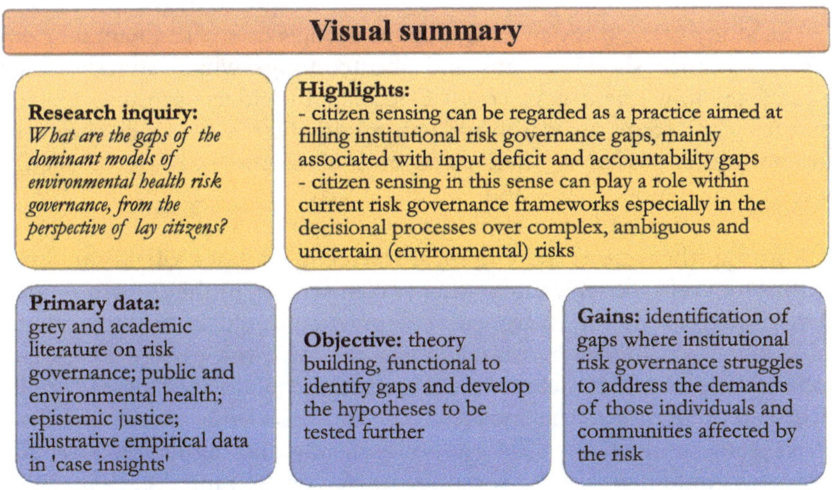

Executive Summary

Grassroots-driven environmental monitoring based on own senses or on sensor technology, i.e., 'citizen sensing', can be considered a constructive response to crises. When lay people distrust official information or just want to fill data gaps, they may resort to sensors and data infrastructures to visualize, monitor and report risks caused by environmental factors to public health. Although through frictions with the institutions or with other stakeholders, citizen sensing may ultimately have the potential to contribute to institutional risk governance as the discussed *Safecast* case of citizen sensing targeting post-Fukushima radiation monitoring, demonstrate.

The book provides novel insights, exploring the potential for the 'sensing citizens' to concretely influence risk governance by filling—intentional or accidental—official informational gaps. Citizen sensing proves to be a practice able to address governance challenges in the way data over a (environmental) risk problem are gathered and provided to the public. This essentially unveils the issue of a perceived legitimacy gap in current (environmental) risk governance. Nonetheless, it also opens avenues for a more inclusive and transparent governmental response to complex risks.

The study offers a review of dominant models of environmental health risk governance showing gaps and shortcomings which stimulated an inquiry on how these gaps may be tackled by citizen sensing. Citizen sensing often stems from dissatisfaction and distrust towards the institutional system of risk governance and from the need to challenge informational monopolies and dogmatic ways of governing risks. This trend is investigated in the book through empirical analyses.

Through theoretical and empirical research, the book offers the foundations for constructively integrating citizen sensing in the current models of risk governance. It is argued that practice could contribute to the achievement of a more accountable and inclusive risk governance, especially in case of highly debated, ambiguous and politicized risks. Despite identified limitations, the inclusion of the knowledge stemming from citizen sensing practices to inform policymaking and regulations over risk problems could increase the social legitimacy of such interventions.

Contents

1	**Introduction**	1
2	**The Concepts of Public and Environmental Health Risk Governance: Hidden Controversies in Apparently Plain Notions**	7
	Public and Environmental Health	8
	Public Health	8
	Environmental Health	13
	Risk and Environmental Risk to Public Health	22
	The Notion of Risk	22
	Risk Categories	30
	Risk Attributes	33
	The Importance of Risk Perception	36
	Definitions of Risk in Practice	40
	Governance and Risk Governance	42
	References	48
3	**Identifying Dominant Models of Environmental Health Risk Governance**	57
	Dominant Models According to Millstone	57
	Weber and Durkheim's Decisionist Model	60
	The Technocratic Model	60
	The Inverted Decisionist Model	60
	The Co-dynamic Model	61

Reading the Models Through Three Questions 62
The Gaps and Shortcomings of the Described Models 69
References 77

4 Hypothesizing a New Approach to Risk Governance Based on Citizen Sensing 81
The Role of Expert and Lay Knowledge in Current Risk Governance 82
Theory of Change: How Citizen Sensing Can Contribute to Risk Governance 88
Theoretical Justifications for Including Citizen Sensing in Institutional Risk Governance 98
References 109

5 Conclusion 115
Key Takeaways From the Study 116
Limitations of the Study 120
References 122

Index 125

About the Author

Anna Berti Suman is Assistant Professor (tenure track) in Environmental Law & Sociology at the University of Padua. Between 2023 and 2025, she was Senior Researcher in Sustainable Innovation & Public Law at Luiss University, Law School, Rome, and she served as Head of Research at LabGov—Laboratory for the Governance of the Commons. Between 2020 and 2023, she was Marie Skłodowska-Curie Individual Fellowship grantee and Dutch Research Council postdoctoral fellow at the European Commission's Joint Research Centre, Ispra, Italy. She founded and still curates the "Sensing for Justice" project aimed at exploring the potential of civic monitoring as a source of evidence for environmental litigation and as a tool to foster environmental mediation. She is also Qualified Barrister, admitted to the Bar of Rome, following climate and environmental law cases for various NGOs, including A Sud—Ecology and Cooperation, Rome, and Systasis—Centre for the Prevention and Management of Environmental Conflicts, Milan. She obtained her Ph.D. in 2020 after a four-year trajectory at the Tilburg Institute for Law, Technology & Society, The Netherlands. Her Ph.D. project aimed at investigating how civic monitoring influences the governance of environmental health risk and how the practice can be integrated within institutional models of risk governance. She has a background in Law from the University of Bologna with a specialization in Transnational Law from the University of Geneva. She has work and research experience in environmental litigation (Italy, The Netherlands, Ecuador), water law (Chile) and health law (UK). She published peer-reviewed articles, policy briefs and books that generated high academic interest, policy influence and social impact. She has been invited to present her results in more than 50 guest presentations and keynotes at prestigious, international scientific venues. In 2025, she obtained a competitive €1.3 million grant for the project "PersoNa—Personal Narratives in climate litigation" awarded by the Italian Science Fund. In 2024, she featured in the Top 2% Most Influential Scientists ranking by Stanford University and Elsevier, and her milestone book "Civic Monitoring for Environmental Law Enforcement" was published by Edward Elgar. In 2023, she received the European Commission's Young Scientist Award and her work featured on Nature Sustainability. In 2022, she earned the "Science Engagement Breakthrough of the Year" title at the Falling Walls Science Summit, Berlin.

LinkedIn page: https://www.linkedin.com/in/anna-berti-suman-439359132/

"Sensing for Justice" project web page: https://sensingforjustice.webnode.it/

Research identifier and publications: https://orcid.org/0000-0002-8973-8436

Abbreviations

DPIA	Data Protection Impact Assessment
DRM	Disaster Risk Management
DRR	Disaster Risk Reduction
EU	European Union
FAO	UN Food and Agriculture Organization
GDPR	General Data Protection Regulation
IAEA	International Atomic Energy Agency
IEHIA	Integrated Environmental Health Impact Assessment
IRGC	International Risk Governance Council
JRC	European Commission's Joint Research Centre
OECD	Organization of Economic Cooperation and Development
OHSAS	Occupational Health & Safety Advisory Services
RIVM	Dutch Institute for Public Health and the Environment
SARF	Social Amplification of Risk Framework
STS	Science and Technology Studies
TEPCO	Tokyo Electric Power Company
UK	United Kingdom
UN	United Nations
US	United States
WBGU	German Advisory Council on Global Change
WHO	World Health Organization

List of Figures

Fig. 2.1	Approaches to the analysis of risk	30
Fig. 2.2	From uncertain, ambiguous and complex problems to citizen sensing	40
Fig. 2.3	A working definition of environmental risk to public health	43
Fig. 2.4	Risk governance at the intersection of the debate on risk and on governance	45
Fig. 3.1	A critical analysis of Weber and Durkheim's decisionist model	62
Fig. 3.2	A critical analysis of the technocratic model	62
Fig. 3.3	A critical analysis of the inverted decisionist model	63
Fig. 3.4	A critical analysis of the co-dynamic model	63
Fig. 3.5	Linear versus non-linear models of risk governance	65
Fig. 4.1	Citizen sensing 'fit' in the IRGC Risk Governance Process (IRGC 2005, 65)	91
Fig. 4.2	Clash and convergence of citizen sensing in the current models of risk governance (Berti Suman 2018b, 269)	97
Fig. 4.3	Mutual contribution between grassroots and institutional risk governance	100

Case Insights

Case Insight	1: Public and Environmental Health Risk Governance in the Chernobyl Disaster	46
Case Insight	2: Scepticism Towards Traditional Approaches in Governing Risks	75
Case Insight	3: Making Risk Governance More Horizontal	106
Case Insight	4: Creating Spaces for Reactive Citizen Science	118

List of Tables

Table 2.1 Definitions of public health and related criticisms 14
Table 2.2 Definitions of environmental health and related criticisms 19

CHAPTER 1

Introduction

Abstract The Introduction lays down the foundations to build a theoretical frame in which citizen sensing for environmental risk monitoring will be discussed in light of selected doctrinal discussions from risk governance doctrine. The chapter essentially is a problem statement as it targets citizen sensing in relation to the issue of a perceived legitimacy gap in current (environmental) risk governance. Developing the sociological argument that citizen sensing may respond to a legitimacy crisis in risk governance, the Introduction can be considered the foundation for the research developed in the next chapters. Prior to exploring a potential contribution of citizen sensing to risk governance, it is worth to inquire whether current institutional risk governance needs adaptations. Furthermore, the chapter engages in a reflection on the legitimacy of a possible contribution from citizen sensing initiatives.

Keyword Citizen sensing · Legitimacy · Crisis · Risk governance

The present contribution introduces the foundations of citizen sensing for environmental risk monitoring. This background will later be used to build a theoretical frame and to structure a discussion from the risk governance perspective. The book essentially represents a problem statement in the sense that it targets citizen sensing in relation to the issue of a perceived *legitimacy gap* in current (environmental) risk governance. It

A. Berti Suman, *Citizen Sensing for Risk Response*,
https://doi.org/10.1007/978-3-032-03939-2_1

develops the sociological argument that citizen sensing may respond to a legitimacy crisis in risk governance. Indeed, the analysis of a potential contribution from citizen sensing to risk governance through its policy uptake requires, beforehand, an inquiry on whether current institutional risk governance actually needs adaptations, and on the legitimacy of a possible contribution from citizen sensing initiatives.

The book has a tripartite structure, each step corresponding to a chapter. First, the key elements of the problem (public and environmental health; risk and environmental health risk; governance and risk governance) are disentangled in Chapter 2, which discusses these key concepts as isolated notions as well as in their interplay. The concepts are problematized through the juxtaposition of definitions formulated from different standpoints, i.e., the institutional and the academic. For example, the notions of environmental health and public health are criticized through the voices of diverging opinions expressing criticisms (i.e., over-simplification, bias) that unveil inherent conflicts in notions presented as 'standards'. The observant reader will note that a more thorough analysis is devoted to the notion of risk and its governance as it is essentially from risk scholarship that the key problem statement of this book is extracted. In Chapter 3, the 'problem' itself and its state-of-the-art are discussed by investigating the arguably dominant models of environmental risk governance and their criticisms. Particular attention is devoted to the discussion on the role of expert and lay knowledge in current risk governance. Thirdly, throughout Chapter 4, a 'theory of change' is outlined by hypothesizing a new approach to risk governance based on citizen sensing, and by inspecting its theoretical grounding and the need for empirical analysis. At the end of the book, conclusive reflections are developed.

The central contribution that this book offers is the argument that prevailing models of environmental risk governance often *fail* to include the input of the concerned stakeholders. This acknowledgement stimulates me to suggest that participatory practices of risk monitoring such as citizen sensing may—on one side—improve people's trust in risk policy and decision-making and—on the other side—effectively strengthen the ability of society to cope with complex risks. The conceptualization that follows (Chapter 2) provides the working language for understanding the problem addressed by this research. However, it is also functional to the analysis of the criticisms to the dominant models of risk governance (Chapter 3) and to the theory of change (Chapter 4).

The book embraces a mixed-methods approach adopted to target the research aim, combining theory review with empirical data collection based on expert interviews and case study-based ethnography. The data collection strategy used for this book has been based on a review of academic literature on the relevant concepts and theories. In addition, policy documents and statements available on official websites of organizations dealing with environmental health and risks have been consulted. The observant reader will note that the first part of the book is mostly based on relatively older literature, whereas the more the book proceeds towards the theory of change the more recent the literature becomes. This is due to the need to first conceptualize rather 'old' concepts such as public and environmental health and then dive into more recent discussions on risk governance. Overall, the desk research has been guided by exploratory consultations that I had with experts in the field, both from academia and from institutions.

Furthermore, the literature review has been complemented by three in-depth, semi-structured, face-to-face interviews, performed in 2018.[1] The experts consulted come from the policy sector and from academia, respectively an expert of Risk Governance and an expert of Citizen Science from the Dutch Institute for Public Health and the Environment (RIVM), and an expert of Responsible Innovation and of Urban Innovation theories from Delft University of Technology. These experts have been contacted to get a first impression on views from the institutional arena and from the academic sector about the potential of citizen sensing for environmental risk governance, within the framework of innovation in governance of environmental and public health issues. The theoretical framework was applied to structure the interviews and to stay alerted on key factors (such as the mention of crucial concepts, i.e., distrust), that then played a key role in analysing the results and inserting them in such a frame, also with an eye to refining and enriching it with aspects that may have been overlooked.

[1] The interviews lasted approximately 1.5 hours each and two out of three were recorded and transcribed with permission. For the one without recording and transcription, field notes are available. In addition, for all the three interviews, summaries were made for the purposes of this book and are available upon request. The agreements made with the interviewees entail the disclosure of the function but not of the name of the experts interviewed. The interviewees are granted access to the piece as incorporating their statements. This section of the research has been granted ethical clearance by the Ethical Review Board of Tilburg Law School (TLS-ERB #2018/01 issued on June 12, 2018).

'Case insights' boxes with selected extracts based on responses collected from volunteers of citizen sensing projects (illustrative, comparative case studies) complement the analysis, based on the results of an online questionnaire and follow-up interviews performed in 2019–2020,[2] and of field ethnography performed in 2020–2021.[3] I opted for bringing in an empirical angle to the discussion as I deemed it worthwhile to have the perspective of the people engaged in citizen sensing expressed also here. The theory also here became the guidance to build the questionnaire script and to shape the fieldwork plan. In addition, it served for constructing the code applied to analyse the obtained results.

[2] Also this part of the research and in particular the online questionnaire administered with Qualtrics has been granted ethical clearance by the Ethical Review Board of Tilburg Law School (TLS-ERB #2018/01 issued on June 12, 2018).

[3] The field research in Basilicata received ethical clearance by the Research Ethics Board of the European Commission Joint Research Centre in August 2020.

CHAPTER 2

The Concepts of Public and Environmental Health Risk Governance: Hidden Controversies in Apparently Plain Notions

Abstract This chapter has a tripartite structure, each step corresponding to a section and sub-sections. This tripartite structure mirrors the three key elements of the problem that this book aims to tackle: public and environmental health; risk and environmental health risk; governance and risk governance. These key notions shape the problem of (perceived) legitimacylegitimacy and accountability gaps in the governance of environmental risks to public health. In the chapter, these notions are described as isolated concepts as well as in their interplay. These concepts are problematized through the juxtaposition of definitions formulated from different standpoints, i.e., the institutional and the academic. Arguably 'reference notions', such as that of environmental health and public health, are criticized through the voices of diverging opinions expressing criticisms (i.e., over-simplification, biases). The discussion of these notions sets the scene for the research that follows and unveils inherent conflicts in notions presented as the reference.

Keywords Public health · Environmental health · Risk governance · Reference notions

A. Berti Suman, *Citizen Sensing for Risk Response*,
https://doi.org/10.1007/978-3-032-03939-2_2

Public and Environmental Health

Public Health

This book unpacks the problem of (perceived) legitimacy and accountability gaps in the governance of environmental risks to public health. Throughout this research project, I have investigated whether practices of citizen sensing could be (part of) a possible solution. In order to define the problem and its boundaries, I decided to start with setting the scene for environmental risks to public health. This section responds to this need by inspecting the meaning of the concepts underlying the problem. It starts with defining the intertwined concepts of environmental health, public health and risk. Where appropriate, the 'dominant' definitions of such concepts are criticized and hints to the problem identified, i.e., legitimacy and accountability gaps in environmental risk governance, are advanced.

From the formulation 'environmental risk(s) to public health' derives that the domain of environmental health is here considered in its intersection with public health. Environmental health has been defined as a 'branch'[1] of public health targeting the factors in the natural and built environment that may affect human health. As environmental health in this study is regarded as a sub-domain of public health, it seems worthwhile to outline first the broader concept of public health in order to subsequently move to the more specific notion of environmental health. The phrasing 'environmental risk(s) to public health' is adopted to stress a limitation of scope: not all environmental risks are considered in this research, but just those potentially posing a threat to public health; not all public health issues are addressed, but only those deriving from environmental risks. The reader will often find the construct 'environmental risk(s) to public health' abbreviated as 'environmental (health) risk(s)'. The two constructs are here used interchangeably. Over the book, I will refer in short to 'environmental risk' and 'environmental risk governance'

[1] The characterization of Environmental Health as a branch of Public Health can be referred back to the '90s and in particular to 1997 when the U.S. Agency for Toxic Substances and Disease Registry released the following definition: "Environmental health is *the branch of public health* that protects against the effects of environmental hazards that can adversely affect health or the ecological balances essential to human health and environmental quality". For an historical overview of the developments of the concept in the U.S. scenario see https://health.gov/environment/DefinitionsofEnvHealth/ehdef2.htm#7.

yet referring only to a *subset* of the whole range of possible environmental risks, that is, those affecting public health.

Starting with an institutional definition of public health provided from the World Health Organization (WHO), 'public health' would be "the art and science of preventing disease, prolonging life and *promoting health* through *the organized efforts of society*" [emphasis added] (WHO website[2]; Acheson 1988). This reference to the 'organized efforts' would suggest that a series of measures are planned and adopted in a conventional way to promote health. The organizational component recalls an institutional division of competences with regards to who oversees what in ensuring health promotion. Yet, the mention of 'society' in an unspecified manner seems suggesting that promoting health is a burden shared by the *whole* society, thus including both the institutions responsible for health and the citizens whose health is at issue. I support this latter interpretation as participatory methods such as citizen sensing could be ultimately justified by this sense of shared responsibility in addressing public health problems, as also emerged from the analysis contained in the case insight titled "Making risk governance more horizontal".

The WHO definition follows stating that "public health focuses on the *entire spectrum of health and wellbeing*, not only the eradication of particular diseases" [emphasis added]. The goal is "to provide conditions under which people can maintain to be healthy or improve their health and wellbeing or prevent the deterioration of their health. This is done by activities to strengthen public health capacities and service" (WHO website[3]; Acheson 1988). This holistic approach to health is endorsed in light of the circumstance that most of the risks discussed here do not (directly) lead to a specific disease but rather endanger the broader health and wellbeing of the affected people.

The notion of public health, as framed by the WHO, has been heavily contested by relevant academic literature (*infra*) because claimed to be too simplistic and optimistic. Paul Hunt, Former United Nations (UN) Special Rapporteur on the right to the highest attainable standard of health, in office between 2002 and 2008, during a public speech delivered at the 2018 IUCN Academy of Environmental Law Colloquium

[2] WHO website: http://www.euro.who.int/en/health-topics/Health-systems/public-health-services/public-health-services.

[3] Ibid.

"The Transformation of Environmental Law and Governance", argued that this definition might be in need of revisions.[4] A number of criticisms in fact surrounds the WHO notion. First of all, phrasings such as that public health represents "the art and science of [...] prolonging life and promoting health" and entails "provid[ing] conditions under which people can maintain to be healthy or improve their health" (WHO website[5]; Acheson 1988) suggest a 'promotional' approach to health. Such an approach seems pervaded by a *top-down* division in which the top (institutions in charge of public health) provides to the people the conditions to be healthy. The responsibility of the individuals to take care of their health themselves, widely discussed by Polzer and Power (2016) with regards to health in the Neoliberal Governance, appears underplayed. Moreover, the potential of the unique knowledge of the people—either lay citizens or patients—in addressing their health is disregarded (one may think, for example, of Indigenous communities' wisdom in how to cure diseases with products of the nature). In the WHO notion as it is, there seems to be limited room for participatory practices of public health governance such as citizen sensing. At the end of this section and through the analysis of literature contesting the WHO definition, I will suggest a working definition of public health in which practices of citizen sensing and similar initiatives may eventually play a role.

In the academic literature, it has been stressed that public health is essentially a political notion. The political dimension of public health has been stressed by Gostin (2000), who defines public health as:

> The legal powers and duties of the state to assure the conditions for people to be healthy, and the limitations on the power of the state to constrain the autonomy, privacy, liberty, proprietary, or other legally protected interests of individuals for the protection or promotion of community health.

Gostin embraces both the positive (the power and duties to...) and the negative obligations' dimensions (the limitations on the power to...) of the institutional action in the promotion of public health. On one side,

[4] Statement made during the 2018 IUCN Academy of Environmental Law Colloquium which I attended, "The Transformation of Environmental Law and Governance: Innovation, Risk and Resilience", Glasgow, July 4–6, 2018.

[5] WHO website: http://www.euro.who.int/en/health-topics/Health-systems/public-health-services/public-health-services.

this again seems a very hierarchical definition. On the other side, the mention of individual autonomy gives arguably a role to *personal responsibility* in taking care of one's own health (by means—for example—of practices such as those discussed here). In fact, top-down, hierarchical approaches in addressing public health may not be in contrast with a 'responsibilization' of the individual. For instance, the 'governmentality' approach as originally developed by Foucault (1991) and elaborated further by other scholars, postulates that "processes of *governing, subjectification and responsibility-taking* are closely interlinked" [emphasis added] (Pyysiäinen, Halpin and Guilfoyle 2017, 216). This literature defends that the action of the state is facilitated or even enabled by "the establishment of a form of subjectivity or self-hood—such as an 'enterprising self'" (Rose 1992) through which an agent "would produce the ends of government by fulfilling themselves rather than being merely obedient" (Rose, O'Malley, and Valverde 2006; as cited in Pyysiäinen, Halpin and Guilfoyle 2017, 216). This argument clearly blurs the boundaries between what is responsibility-taking as a form of emancipation (linking this concept to Beck's notion of emancipatory catastrophe, Beck 2015) and autonomous decision, and responsibilization as a means to 'be governed'.

The reflections of Gostin on values that interplay with the concept of public health, such as autonomy, privacy and liberty, have been endorsed by Oliver (2006) who reflects on the moral judgments involved in the art and science of protecting public health and the *legitimacy* these judgements gain on the political debate due to effects of democratic processes. Democracy would be, according to Oliver (2006), highly intertwined with the sense of legitimacy and thus the acceptance of public health judgements and decisions. Democracy and legitimacy will be at the core of the present discussion, as citizen sensing intrinsically link with both concepts.

Srinivasan, O'Fallon and Dearry (2003) complemented the WHO definition stressing the importance of considering both physical and mental health problems in the notion of public health. In addition, they connected physical and mental health to the built environment, including human-modified places such as homes, schools, workplaces, parks, industrial areas, farms, roads and highways. These interlinks seem particularly timely in today's reality of highly urbanized societies. The creation of health-promoting environments or, in other words, encouraging health via urban strategies has been suggested also by Frank and Engelke (2001, 215) as one of the ways to promote public health 'in the city'. Timely to this research, Haines et al. (2005, 593) suggested a broader definition of public health also including issues related to climate change. The authors underlined the causal link between consequences of climate change (e.g., heat weaves) and the ailments (such as fatigue and even heart attacks) especially affecting the elderly as particularly vulnerable subjects. Public health decision-makers are encouraged by the authors to take into account the consequences of climate change in their policies and adopt adaptation strategies in the longer term (e.g., climate education and heat waves warning systems).

Along this line, the strong interdependency of public health and environmental health (Wu et al. 2007), bridging the public health discussion with the domain of environmental risk monitoring, has been underlined. The environmental dimension of public health is here considered as comprising both outdoor and indoor environments. Whereas the connection of public health with the outdoor environment is undiscussed, only recently the impact of indoor environmental quality on public health became a matter of growing concern. This because people today spend on average more than 90% of their time indoors (Wu et al. 2007). Again, education and adaptation strategies seem crucial to tackle the issue (Wu et al. 2007).

In conclusion, it can be argued that public health is a highly political notion which has been criticized and reshaped and will constantly evolve on the basis of new debates in the field. In spite of the illustrated controversial nature of the WHO notion, the definition appears *partially* appropriate for this research for the connection it establishes between promoting health and the 'efforts of society', here considered in a broad sense as not only comprising those professionals explicitly responsible for promoting public health (e.g., medical sector, public health ministries, health researchers, etc.), but also non-professional members of the civil society (auto-)organized for preventing or facing a public health problem.

Nonetheless, I suggest amending the WHO definition in view of the inclusion not only of physical but also an explicit reference to mental health. This would be in line of the mentioned WHO's phrasing in the definition of public health as "the entire spectrum of health and well-being" and the WHO definition of health itself as "a state of complete physical, mental and social wellbeing and not merely the absence of disease or infirmity" (WHO 1948). In addition, the role of individuals as active player in improving public (and personal) health must be acknowledged. Furthermore, the link between public health and environmental health (in the sense describe above) must be taken into account in consideration that environmental factors—as air pollution and heat waves—are increasingly impacting public health. Lastly, the *legitimacy* of those institutions in charge for taking decisions to protect public health should be at the core of the discussion and new avenues to make their decision-making more accountable and participatory need to be explored.

A working definition of public health, based on the discussed literature, is the following: "public health is the practice of promoting both physical and mental health through the synergy of the whole society, including the individuals (lay citizens or patients) as active players in the debate and in concrete actions. Public health encompasses also the prevention of those environmental risks impacting on human health and the governance thereof". The discussed perspectives on the concept of public health are summarized in Table 2.1.

Environmental Health

Moving from the broader public health domain to the notion of environmental health, a critical definition is again provided. The concept of environmental health, similarly to that of public health, has been inquired and criticized from various perspectives. A definition of environmental health was formulated by the WHO in the early 1990s, which reads as follows [emphasis added] (WHO website)[6]:

> Environmental health addresses all the physical, chemical, and biological factors *external to a person*, and all the related factors impacting behaviours. It encompasses the *assessment* and *control* of those environmental factors that can potentially affect health. [...] [It regards] those aspects of the human health and disease that are determined by factors in the environment [and aims at] preventing disease and creating health-supportive environments. This definition *excludes* behaviour not related to environment, as well as behaviour related to the *social and cultural environment*, and genetics.

This formulation has been scrutinized by both academics and political interest groups in the environmental, health and social welfare sectors.

[6] See http://www.searo.who.int/topics/environmental_health/en/.

Table 2.1 Definitions of public health and related criticisms

Public health		
[WHO definition] "Public health focuses on the entire spectrum of health and wellbeing, not only the eradication of particular diseases". The goal is "to provide conditions under which people can maintain to be healthy or improve their health and wellbeing or prevent the deterioration of their health. This is done by activities to strengthen public health capacities and service" (WHO website; Acheson 1988)	[Criticisms from the literature] The WHO definition suggests a 'promotional' approach to health, pervaded by a top-down approach; the responsibility of the individuals and the potential of their knowledge are underplayed (yet these two approaches could coexist taking a 'governmentaility' perspective); criticisms also include the intrinsically political dimension of 'public health'; the need to consider both physical and mental health problems; the need for a broader definition of public health also including issues related to climate change and stressing the interdependency with environmental health (Gostin 2000; Oliver 2006; Srinivasan et al. 2003; Haines et al. 2005; Wu et al. 2007)	[Working definition] "Public health is the practice of promoting both physical and **mental** health **through the synergy of the whole society**, including the individuals (lay citizens or patients) as active players in the debate and in concrete actions. Public health **encompasses also the prevention of those environmental risks impacting on human health** and the governance thereof."

Among the critiques to the notion the following arguments appear particularly timely to this research: first, the definition embraces *only* the factors external to a person; second, it suggests a prevalently managerial approach to environmental health because it refers to "the assessment and control of those environmental factors"; third, it does *not* account of social and cultural factors (Gee and Payne-Sturges 2004).

Building on Gee and Payne-Sturges (2004), I acknowledge that the understanding of environmental health should incorporate cultural and especially social factors. Disadvantaged communities in poorer areas are more likely to be exposed to ambient hazards than people in wealthier societies, for example, due to poor housing conditions. Furthermore, a minor change in ambient conditions affects poorer communities to a greater extent than richer communities, as the latter can rely on a considerably higher number of resources for mitigating and coping with the consequences of ambient variations. Taking the case of a drought altering the harvest, wealthier sectors of society will have access to mitigation measures (e.g., buying food from elsewhere). Differently, sections of the population with limited financial resources will see their food security highly threatened.

Gee and Payne-Sturges (2004) proposed a constructive critique of the WHO definition. They refer to the Environmental Justice Movement, a social movement originated in the 1970s and 1980s in the U.S., primarily led by African-Americans, Latinos and Native Americans, which advanced the argument that the communities living in the most polluted environments are often racial minorities and poorest people. The Movement suggested the concept of 'psychosocial stress', standing for the vulnerability to environmental hazards to which people living in particularly poor social conditions would be exposed. It is noted that a form of 'environmental racism' would exist, according to which socially marginalized racial minorities would often be exposed to a greater extent to pollutants than more privileged communities. In addition, these minorities would have lower access to sources of ecological benefits (i.e., clean air, water and natural resources).[7] The aggregate effect of underprivileged social conditions and of poor environmental conditions would strongly affect these communities' wellbeing and eventually increase the risk of illnesses (Gee and Payne-Sturges 2004).

In addition, Gee and Payne-Sturges (2004) refer to a form of 'residential segregation' meaning urban agglomerates with low socio-environmental and living conditions, which may produce *differential experiences* of exposure to pollutants and access to common resources such as green and recreational areas. This residential segregation could alter *substantially* the level of community stress in relation to environmental factors. For example, people living in slums may be exposed to the same level of air pollution than people living in city centres, but may suffer it more heavily than the second dwellers as they cannot rely on a wealth of green areas or do not have the means to leave the city for spending

[7] For the Environmental Justice Movement see Pellow et al. (2001).

few days in the countryside where the air is cleaner. Consequently, they will experience air pollution more severely.

I align with Gee and Payne-Sturges (2004) in arguing that these disparities in how environmental health is perceived, both a collective and at an individual level, need to be take into account and counterbalanced through targeted actions. A definition such as the WHO's that disregards socio-cultural stressors miss a crucial part of the problem, i.e., that different socio-cultural contexts differently shape public and environmental health challenges. Not considering the described *systemic factors* leading to a heightened vulnerability to environmental risks may determine the failure or unexpected outcomes of interventions. Consequently, environmental health promotion should not only tackle environmental health challenges *strictu* sensu but should also entail policies aimed at eliminating or at least reducing those social stressors (Gee and Payne-Sturges 2004). The cases investigated in this research will be analysed by considering both physical and social factors that determine an environmental stressor. Although citizen sensing so far has been a predominantly Western phenomenon, yet some outstanding examples are spreading in developing countries with remarkable results.[8] Nonetheless, the reality of extreme conditions (where, for example, an Internet connection is not available) will not be captured in this research.

It should be also noted that scientists are moving from a narrow understanding of environmental health, i.e., focusing on toxic substances and their relationship to human illnesses, to a broader study of the effects on human health of both the physical and the *social* environment, which includes issues related to urban and rural development, industrial development, public transportation, appropriate use of land etc. (Srinivasan et al. 2003). Dickinson and Iles (2017), for example, include in the environmental health sciences the study of such factors outside the body, impacting (long term) overall health of the public, that span from food, water and air, but also physical (interestingly, e.g., radiation), biologicals, chemicals and *social agents* such as violence and depression. Even more remarkably, the authors suggest that a lens for examining environmental health issues is that of an environmental justice discourse. The recognition of a *psychosocial component* has also been pointed out by relevant authors (Yassi et al. 2001) according to which environmental health risks

[8] For an account of citizen sensing phenomenon in developing countries, see the work of Georgiadou (for example Georgiadou et al. 2014).

range from biological, chemical, physical, biomechanical and psychosocial etc. Literature (Stephens and Church 2017) also referred to key components for a healthy environment people's access to not only physical and economic resources, but also aesthetic, mental and spiritual needs, such as green space and quiet. This attention to social, psychosocial and spiritual determinants also in relation to the notion of environmental health is here endorsed.

Also with regard to the WHO definition of environmental health, the academic literature has suggested that the importance of indoor environmental conditions is underplayed. Adamkiewicz et al. (2011), for example, developed a theoretical and empirical framework aimed at planning strategies to tackle environmental health issues connected with indoor environmental risks. The authors elaborate on the circumstance that indoor pollution would be particularly high in low-socioeconomic status households due to a combination of influences of indoor sources of pollution (such as wood and coal heating, and low-quality cooking appliances), outdoor sources (such as pollution from nearby factories) and residential activity patterns (such as tobacco consumption and sedentary lifestyles), coupled with specific characteristics of low-income residences (e.g., air-leakages).

The importance of integrating several aspects in the notion of environmental health, thus going beyond the narrow WHO definition, is stressed by the supporters of the Integrated Environmental Health Impact Assessment (IEHIA) approach. Lebret (2016, 1) defines IEHIA as "an element in the third phase of environmental risk management [which] focuses on providing *inclusive descriptions* of *multiple impacts* from *multiple stressors* in such a way that they can be evaluated against the potential societal benefits of the causes of the stressors" [emphasis added]. The technique is essentially aimed at assessing health-related risks deriving from environmental factors and evaluating associated policies and other interventions taking into account the *complexities, interdependencies and uncertainties* of such risks (Briggs 2008). This idea interestingly recalls the characterization of 'risk' discussed later in this section.

Lastly, over the years the need to assign indicators to the concept of environmental health has been perceived widely aimed at facilitating the design of policy interventions (Dalbokova and Krzyzanowski 2002). In the political arena, the WHO European Centre for Environment and Health is implementing an indicator system on the basis of an internationally agreed methodology and comparable standards (Briggs 2008).

The system, intended to be a standard framework for the assessment of environmental health issues, has been criticized as being *too linear*, top-down and missing social aspects. This once again shows a tension, relevant for the present discussion, between an institutional way of dealing with environmental health issues through the imposition of categories and schemes, and a push for a more social context-driven response to the problem. Various alternatives to these indicators have been proposed, emphasizing the importance of *contextual* factors as key determinants of exposure, susceptibility and health impact (Briggs 2008).

Building on the discussed perspectives, it can be concluded that 'environmental health', as already observed for 'public health', is a scientific, social and also a political notion. The institutional definition from the WHO focuses on its scientific meaning (all the physical, chemical and biological factors external to a person) and managerial meaning (the assessment and control of those environmental factors that can potentially affect health). The political and managerial meaning is also evident in the adoption of environmental health indicators through which environmental health is targeted as a management problem. Following the reasoning of the academic literature presented, it can be argued that the WHO definition should be complemented with the inclusion of the concept of psychosocial stressors affecting environmental health experiences and with hints to the impact on health of indoor environmental conditions. I support the argument that environmental health policies should target not only the physical, chemical and biological factors external to a person, but also and most importantly all those contextual factors and social stressors affecting the experience of environmental health. Social and economic factors thus act as mediating factors, which can magnify or reduce the problem, but are not per se the cause of the problem.

As for public health, here a working definition of environmental health is provided. In light of the previous discussion, environmental health can be defined as including "the physical, chemical, and biological factors present both in the outdoor and in the indoor environment, as well as the psychosocial stressors external to a person that affect their health" and meaning also "the practice of assessing, controlling and managing these factors as well as the personal experiencing of such factors". The discussed perspectives on environmental health are summarized in Table 2.2.

I wish to add that, although both the concepts of environmental health and of public health have always been a pressing concern for public policy

Table 2.2 Definitions of environmental health and related criticisms

Environmental health		
[WHO definition] "Environmental health addresses all the physical, chemical, and biological factors external to a person, and all the related factors impacting behaviours. It encompasses the assessment and control of those environmental factors that can potentially affect health. [It regards] those aspects of the human health and disease that are determined by factors in the environment. [...] It is targeted towards preventing disease and creating health-supportive environments. This definition excludes behaviour not related to environment, as well as behaviour related to the social and cultural environment, and genetics" (WHO website)	[Criticisms from the literature] The WHO definition embraces only the factors external to a person; it suggests a managerial approach to environmental health as it refers to "the assessment and control of those environmental factors"; it does not account for social and cultural factors as key determinants of exposure, susceptibility and health impact; lastly the importance of indoor environmental conditions are underplayed (Gee and Payne-Sturges 2004; Dalbokova and Krzyzanowski 2002; Srinivasan et al. 2003; Adamkiewicz et al. 2011; Briggs 2008)	[Working definition] "Environmental health can be defined as including the physical, chemical, and biological factors present **both in the outdoor and in the indoor environment as well as the psychosocial stressors** external to a person that affect her/his health and meaning also the practice of assessing, controlling and managing these factors as well as the **personal experiencing** of such factors"

and society, their importance for policy-making increased after the Second World War. As Bates (1994, 4) notes, the catastrophic events of the war led to the rise of several environmental hazards challenging the already weakened public health. Little known issues like asbestos, the worrying exposure to air pollution (for example, the 1952 London smog episode) and the noxious effects of electromagnetic fields due to the development of high voltage transmission lines, became major concerns over the decades following the end of the war. The rate of cancer, lung diseases and cardiac diseases associated with exposure to pollutants, chemicals, radiations and fine dusts reached its peak after the war, resting approximately steady until current days (Bates 1994, 4).

These developments show how technological progress—ranging from high voltage, use of lead in gasoline, the boom of the car industry etc.—contributed to the decrease of public health in post-war society (Berti Suman 2018b). According to Bates (1994), these factors turned to be pressing menaces for society as the level of exposure, although low, affected a considerable number of people. Rose argues (1989, 349–356) that a low level of exposure for a very large section of population is a more serious public health concern than a high level of exposure for a small group.[9] The lesson of this statement is that the breadth of the impact of environmental factors on population substantially increased after the Second World War, making environmentally related diseases and ailments a growing concern for public policies.

This reflection highlights a link between environmental health issues, post-war industrialization and technological developments. Human progress, especially in the decades following the Second World War, has indeed often been achieved at the cost of environmental health conditions. If before the war an epidemiological understanding of environmental health (often related to poor living conditions and sanitation) was dominant, the post-war era has been afflicted by man and technology-caused diseases, such as lung cancer, emphysema and heart diseases linked to chemicals and air pollution (Jackson 1996; Laakkonen et al. 2017; also discussed in Berti Suman 2018b).

Whereas in the 'agricultural society' infectious diseases,[10] such as cholera, were the first environmental health concerns, in the 'industrial society', air, water and noise pollution became pressing threat for public health as a consequence of migration from the countryside to fast growing towns and cities where factories were located (Hobsbawm 1969). It is worth quoting Hobsbawm (1969, 86), who affirms: "And what cities! ... smoke hung over them and filth impregnated them, [...] and an appalling constant toll of the two great groups of nineteenth century *urban killers—air pollution and water pollution* or respiratory [...] disease" [emphasis added]. The Second World War itself had massive social and environmental impacts and left a legacy that Laakkonen, Tucker and Vuorisalo (2017) framed as "the Long Shadow" of the war on global environmental conditions. Later on, in the technological 'risk society', environmental health became mostly challenged by issues related to

[9] This view may be contested by those standing for the small group.

[10] Yet, the COVID-19 pandemic that the world is currently experiencing may suggest a 'return to the past'.

climate change, ozone depletion, chemical pollution and nuclear disasters (Jackson 1996).

The scope of this research does not include the traditional hazards of the pre-war society, e.g., poor sanitation and hygiene, and rather focuses on the consequences of modern society (agricultural and industrial contamination of air, water, food and land; air pollution; nuclear radiations; climate change etc.) on public and environmental health. The effects of such environmental hazards relevant here are as diverse as their nature, ranging from catastrophic direct effects (e.g., the chemical poisoning outbreak in Bhopal, India), to chronic effects (e.g., the severe mercury poisoning in Minamata, Japan), to subtle, indirect and even disputed effects (e.g., the dumping of toxic waste in Love Canal, USA) (Berti Suman 2018a). This book will not address all the possible environmental risks to public health. On the contrary, the focus will be on certain risks that have generated the mobilization and self-organization of civil society and have inspired the launch of citizen sensing practices. The nature of the risk will then be considered secondary, as part of the context of the cases studied but not determinant for the choice to analyse an initiative instead of another. As a caveat, it should be reminded that here focus is on the 'dark' side of technological progress, whereas innovation has also contributed to better monitoring, detection and mitigation of many of the risks here discussed, leading to an overall increase in health. Furthermore, citizen sensing too can be considered as a positive result of technological developments.[11]

The link between technological developments and environmental risk to public health is evident. Yet, I try to overturn this negative relationship between technology and environmental health. The technological and social phenomenon discussed here, i.e., citizen sensing, is indeed presented as an *opportunity* for society to use technology positively, with a view to improving societal response to environmental health challenges. One of the goals pursued by this project is to discuss citizen sensing as a 'positive' technology that can actually contribute, rather than endanger, public and environmental health. The practice brings indeed the promise to improve societal response to environmental challenges impacting on public health. Nonetheless, along with its promises, the shortcomings and

[11] See Berti Suman 2020, 'Chapter 2: Setting the scene: what is citizen sensing?'.

challenges of citizen sensing will be discussed and the need for regulation outlined, in view of investigating how citizen sensing can be integrated in the current institutional system for risk governance.

Risk and Environmental Risk to Public Health

The Notion of Risk

The definition of 'risk' is all but uncontested and uncontroversial. As the Australian medical sociologist Deborah Lupton (1993) noted, defining risks is in itself a strategy to alter or maintain the power structure of a given society. Thus, this definition, for its intrinsic relation with power and power structures, deserves particular attention. This section responds to this need by presenting the notion of risks from different standpoints that, both in the academic and in the policy debate, have addressed the topic. Relevant legal and sociological scholarship is explored in the first half of the section, in order to reach a working definition of risk, similarly with what I have already done for the notions of public and environmental health. This literature review will show that, ultimately, the controversies surrounding the definition of risk are just a mirror of the complexity of risk governance.

The first body of scholarship I wish to discuss is the legal doctrine that has contributed to the definition of risk, although often more narrowly focused on the concept of 'risk regulation'. Yet, risk regulation, despite being more legally oriented, has been considered synonymous with risk governance (Renn 2008). Adopting this approach, in this sub-section I refer to 'risk regulation'. In the literature, it has been pointed out how regulation of risk is increasingly shifting to "regulation *through* risk" [emphasis added] (Gellert 2015, 13). Gellert frames this approach as "the risk management of everything" (Gellert 2015, 1) referring to the use of risk and risk management as "methods of regulation" (Gellert 2017, 276) or, in other words, as "a regulatory resource" (Gellert 2017, 288; 2020). This method is evident, according to Gellert (2017, 288; 2020) in how the General Data Protection Regulation 2016/679 (GDPR) deals with risk associated with data processing, requiring data controllers to perform a Data Protection Impact Assessment (DPIA) in case of *high-risk* processing activities, whereas *low* risk data processing does not need it (Art. 35.4 and 35.5 GDPR). This way, the level of riskiness of a typology of data processing is used to define regulatory approaches.

In discussing the use of risk as a method of regulation, the double nature of risk emerges. Risk, in fact, can be framed both as a harm and as an *opportunity* (Power 2007, 28–29). The regulator takes this opportunity using risks as a tool to encourage self-regulatory risk management processes. Interestingly, this frame emerged also in some of the responses collected from citizen sensing participants, where air pollution was characterized not as a risk but as an opportunity for improving environmental conditions and urban policies in the city.

A relevant question at this point would be the interplay between law and risk. Authors, such as Van Dijk, Gellert and Rommetveit (2015), stressed the crucial role of the law in handling risks. They note that, in democratic societies, the law has indisputable *legitimacy* for dealing with risk governance. However, the law may be perceived (e.g., by the citizen sensing participants as those interviewed) as a manifestation of the establishment and of risk governance patters that do not represent the *public*. The concept of 'legitimacy' will recur in this book as citizen sensing will be framed (also) as a *legitimate* way to contest the lack of legitimacy of (some) risk management decisions not reflecting the affected people's perspective.

Law and (environmental) risk interplay also in the sense that the mandate of current national and international norms is increasingly that of reducing environmental and health risks through *minimizing exposure* to toxicity through risk management methods (Ricci 2006). Regulatory interventions based on risk assessment and management are expression of a societal decision on "at what cost, past and future hazardous conditions can either be avoided or minimized" (Ricci 2006, 1). Due to limited resources, risk-based methods (or 'regulation through risk' as framed by Gellert 2017, 2020) are fundamental to assess alternatives and make choices, while taking into account *uncertainty* and variability. As noted by Ricci (2006, 1), in this process of risk assessment and management "science and law intersect through legal and scientific causation to the point that the failure to provide a sound causal argument can make an otherwise beneficial law or regulation *invalid*" [emphasis added]. Yet, a question relevant for the present work is which actors are entitled to provide this 'sound causal argument'.

Another relevant debate that has been flourishing in the legal doctrine on risk regards the dichotomy of the traditional 'probability of harm' approach to risk governance *versus* the 'precautionary' approach. The precautionary approach, crystallized in the precautionary principle, arose as a "revolt against the guise of rationality" that have sought to make risk "an objective and rational process" (Quelle unpublished, 3). The principle aims at challenging the assumption that "scientific knowledge is complete, reliable and authoritative enough to base policy on" (Quelle unpublished, 3; Stirling 2007, 309–311). The precautionary approach is expressed in Principle 15 of the Rio Declaration[12] where it is affirmed that epistemic uncertainty "shall not be used as a reason for postponing cost-effective measures" if there are threats of serious or irreversible damage. Along this line, Article 191 of the Treaty on the Functioning of the European Union[13] (EU) affirms that the prevention of harm to human, animal or plant health or the environment can justify the action of EU institutions, in spite of the scientific uncertainty on whether the harm would occur.

The 'harm approach' (on which traditional risk management methods are based) starts from the premise that "the full array of risks is known or, in other words, that all the threats which might arise are identified and that they can be assigned a probability" (Quelle unpublished, 4; Baron 1993). Conversely, the precautionary principle applies when risk assessor concludes that "there is not enough knowledge". In other words, argues Quelle, "the principle entails that possible negative outcomes should be managed, *even if it is not at all* [...] sure [...] whether they might arise" (Quelle unpublished, 4; Steel 2004). Uncertainty is therefore a fundamental component of risks under the precautionary principle. Stirling (2007, 309) captures uncertainty by noting that "*all scientific approaches* are based on the articulation of two fundamental parameters [...] First are things that might happen [...]. Second is the likelihood or probability associated with each. Either of these parameters might be subject to *variously complete or problematic knowledge* [...]" Uncertainty will play

[12] Principle 15: "In order to protect the environment, the precautionary approach shall be widely applied by States according to their capabilities. Where there are threats of serious or irreversible damage, lack of full scientific certainty shall not be used as a reason for postponing cost-effective measures to prevent environmental degradation"; Rio Declaration on Environment and Development (12 August 1992) A/CONF.151/26 Vol. I.

[13] Article 191 TFUE, section 2: "Union policy on the environment shall aim at a high level of protection taking into account the diversity of situations in the various regions of the Union. It shall be based on the *precautionary principle and on the principles that preventive action should be taken,* that environmental damage should as a priority be rectified at source and that the polluter should pay." European Union, Consolidated version of the Treaty on the Functioning of the European Union, 13 December 2007, 2008/C 115/01.

an extremely important role in this research as numerous environmental risks to which citizen sensing responds are (perceived as) uncertain (by the sensing citizens).

As affirmed by Stirling (2007, 312–313), the precautionary principle "points to a rich array of methods that reveal the intrinsically normative and contestable basis for decisions, and the different ways in which our knowledge is *incomplete*" [emphasis added]. These gaps in current knowledge arguably encourage for the inclusion of *other forms* of knowledge production in the debate on risk governance, as for example, lay people knowledge. Quelle (unpublished, 11) defends that, while science and technology scholars already acknowledged the expertise possessed by laypersons, "controllers" (here intended as policy-makers) have to decide "whether or when other (non-scientific) bodies of knowledge or the opinions of laypeople *are also relevant*" [emphasis added].

The precautionary approach over the harm approach seems leaving more room to epistemic uncertainty and laying a possible foundation for the inclusion of lay knowledge in risk governance. This resonates with Irwin's argument (1995, 131), specifically in relation to citizen science, that "*lay knowledges* [...] might enrich decision-making processes and the general *knowledge of hazard and health issues*" [emphasis added]. Yet, Irwin (1995, 131) acknowledges that these 'knowledges' are "currently excluded due to their supposed 'irrationality' and anecdotal nature". Concrete cases of the policy uptake of citizen sensing here discussed demonstrate that this is not always the case.

Moving to the sociological arena, Adams and Niezen (2016, 531) point out the existence of a consensus among sociology scholars on three major perspectives on risk, in spite of the innumerable theories on risk: the Risk Society perspective, the Cultural/Symbolic perspective and the Governmentality perspective. This book mostly aligns with the first perspective which will be consequently analysed more in-depth, although a brief outline of the other two is provided.

Central for the first perspective is the role of the German sociologist Ulrich Beck who coined the term 'Risk Society' in the 1980s. Interestingly, no one before Beck felt the need to characterize society in these terms. Clearly, this does not mean that, before then, society was not confronted with risks. However, what the sociologist captured with the term was the new way in which contemporary society perceived, constructed and responded to risks. According to Beck, the Risk Society represented "a systematic way of dealing with hazards and insecurities induced and introduced by modernisation itself" (Beck 1992, 21). Although 'modernization' is a rather blurry concept, my study embraces the notion as a way to refer to post-industrial society. In addition, and very interestingly for this research, Beck contends that "despite its ubiquity, the meaning of risk remains *indeterminate*. In contemporary society, the effects of various risks are keenly contested by politicians, scientific experts, media professionals and the general public. It is this very lack of consensus that makes risk [...] fascinating [...]; and [...] always likely to produce disagreements" (Beck 2004). Beck, despite providing a unique conceptualization of the Risk Society, seems hesitant in defining 'risk', whereas he focuses on the controversial nature of the notion.

The neologism created by Beck was further developed the British sociologist, Anthony Giddens. Giddens built on the concept of the Risk Society but slightly deviating from Beck's vision to include the notion of 'safety' in the analysis. Giddens (1998, 27–28) affirmed that a risk society is "a society increasingly preoccupied with the future (and also with safety), which generates the notion of risk" [parentheses present in the original text]. In addition, Giddens brings to the fore a distinction particularly relevant to set the scene for this research. The risks to which modern society is exposed would no longer be 'external' to human actions, but 'manufactured risks' (e.g., environmental pollution) that are attributable to the modernization process itself (Giddens 1998). This second type of risks would be characterized by a high level of human agency both in the causation phase of these risks and in the response phase, from which derives the safety obsession of modern society (Giddens 1998).

The Risk Society theory has been revisited by Lupton (2015) in her conceptualization of the 'Digital Risk Society'. In Lupton's view, the Digital Risk Society would be highly intertwined with 'digital surveillance' in the digital era. Accordingly, risk would be "increasingly configured and reproduced by digital media, devices and software" (Adams and Niezen, 2016, 531). Under this angle, digital tools would be simultaneously "mediators of risk" and "sources of new concepts of risk" (Adams and Niezen 2016, 531). Citizen sensing here will be studied both in the sense of mediating (and communicating information on) risks and as a possible source of risks itself.

Rosa, Renn and McCright (2013), in their book "The Risk Society Revisited: Social Theory and Risk Governance", provided another reinterpretation of the Risk Society Theory by situating the societal act of risk handling as a human quest for improved quality of life. Focusing especially on technological and environmental risks, the authors start from the *systemic* nature of these risks, i.e., their embeddedness in a larger context of technological, financial and economic systems, to criticize conventional regulatory processes and suggest new forms of risk assessments. Remarkably, the authors draw on Habermas' communicative action theory (Habermas 1984) to extract the critical notion that dissimilar actors may differentially interpret (framed as 'different consciousness') systemic risks. This acknowledgement calls for more open, participatory and inclusive risk assessment processes, in which citizen sensing seems fitting well.

The focus on the 'consciousness' of the risk creates, in my view, a bridge to Habermas's Theory of Communicative Action, although this theory is not included by Adams and Niezen (2016, 531) in the first perspective on risk. Habermas (1984, 49) distinguishes three worlds: the *objective world*, defined as "the totality of what is the case" about which it is possible to make true propositions (Cecez-Kecmanovic and Janson 1999, 184). Then, he identifies a *social world* consisting of a "normative context that lays down which interactions belong to legitimate interpersonal relations" (Habermas 1984, 88). In the social world, moral practical knowledge is situated under the form of "norms, rules, and values" (Cecez-Kecmanovic and Janson 1999, 184; Habermas 1984). Both worlds are external to an actor, in contrast to the third world identified by Habermas in the *subjective world*, defined "as the totality of subjective experiences to which the actor has privileged access" (Habermas 1984, 100). In the Habermasian frame, this three-world concept represents a reference system for actors engaging in social interactions. Risk can exist in all three worlds, as it implies a real threat, a judgement of value and an individual perception.

In the described frame, Habermas places two typologies of actions, the social actions oriented to success and those oriented to reaching understanding (Cecez-Kecmanovic and Janson 1999, 185; Habermas 1984). The first set of actions implies that actors are mostly interested in achieving a certain goal in the objective world, whereas the second set "seek(s) a communicatively reached *agreement* by relating to the objective, social, and subjective worlds" [emphasis added] (Cecez-Kecmanovic and Janson 1999, 185; Habermas 1984). Habermas coins the term 'communicative actions' referring specifically to such actions oriented to reach a mutual understanding and to simultaneously connect the objective, social and subjective worlds. This goal is achieved by different actors by "negotiating definitions of a situation", by "cooperative interpretation of events, goals, values and norms, and by sharing their subjective experiences, desires and feelings" (Cecez-Kecmanovic and Janson 1999, 185; Habermas 1984).

Such different values, norms and experienceS characterize ambiguous risks. Consequently, reaching a mutual agreement turns to be indispensable for collectively handling this type of risks. This idea resonates with what I will describe further in this book as the Millstone 'co-dynamic' model of risk governance. Communicative action is considered successful when an agreement is achieved and individual interventions are coordinated. This idea is particularly relevant here, as citizen participation in science and policy-making could reconcile different and, at times, opposed worlds with a view to *collectively* facing risks.

The second perspective on risk as identified by Adams and Niezen (2016, 531) is the Cultural/Symbolic, as developed by the British anthropologist Mary Douglas (1970, 1992). According to this perspective, risk analysis would be focused on risk perception and would be shaped by cultural adherence and social learning. In contrast to other theories that rather focus on the economic and cognitive influences on risk perception, this theory defends that that structures of social organization with their embedded cultural and social symbols inject into individuals certain perceptions of risk that reinforce those organizational structures against alternative ones. Under this perspective, the feeling of belonging to a certain social context would heavily shape the understanding and perception of and response to different kinds of risks. For example, a member of an indigenous group would perceive an object daily used in the city as a danger, whereas a city dweller would consider an animal of the forest or a natural event—maybe regarded as inoffensive by the indigenous community—as a threat to life. Following Wildavsky and Dake (1990, 42), the Cultural/Symbolic Theory would be capable to "predict and explain what kind of people will perceive which potential hazards to be how dangerous". Risk perception again emerges as central.

The third perspective, the Governmentality perspective, has been inspired by Foucault's discussion on "historical shifts in social/political power relations" connected to states' desire to "retain [...] control over populations" (Adams and Niezen 2016, 531; Foucault 1991). This perspective is focused on all those methods, such as counting, assessment, categorization and judging/disciplining, that represent mechanisms of (risk) governance and are instrumental to the realization of political programmes or social goals. This perspective emphasizes the 'measuring' component of risk assessment, conducted taking into account both individual and societal perceptions (Adams and Niezen 2016, 531). This measuring and defining, as noted earlier, shape the power structure of a given society (Lupton 1993), in light of a set political agenda, implemented through the exercise of power on individual behaviours (Adams and Niezen 2016, 531). Little space seems left to the role of laypersons in risk governance, as risk handling appears mostly a matter of formalized practices. Under this interpretation, individual choices and behaviours would be shaped by an overarching political will, which clashes with the argument developed here on how individual actions can *steer* political choices, in particular when laypersons enter domains of risk governance formerly belonging exclusively to institutional actors and experts.

Nonetheless, a different way of reading the Governmentality perspective would rather emphasize the role that in Foucault is played by the concept of 'resistance', without which there would be no power. A Pickett (1996, 445) argued, it is not possible to understand Foucault without embracing his concept of resistance. Pickett indeed contests the argument advanced by interpreters of Foucault that the Foucauldian understanding of a disciplinary society paralyzes resistance and revolutionary action. Rather, Pickett (1996) defends that Foucault *always* endorsed the role of resistance as a fundamental form of resistance to power, as would also emerge from Foucault's late piece 'History of Sexuality' (Foucault 1976, transl. 1979) where the relation between power and subjectivity emerges in all its complexity. A quote from the piece illustrates this paradigm: "Where there is power, there is resistance, and yet, or rather consequently, this resistance is never in a position of exteriority in relation to power" (Foucault 1976, transl. 1979, 95). This second interpretation would align more the Governmentality perspective on risk with the aims of this research for the role it devotes to resistance. I will indeed demonstrate that citizen sensing can be read as a form of resistance to power structures.

The three perspectives on risk just discussed are summarized in Fig. 2.1.

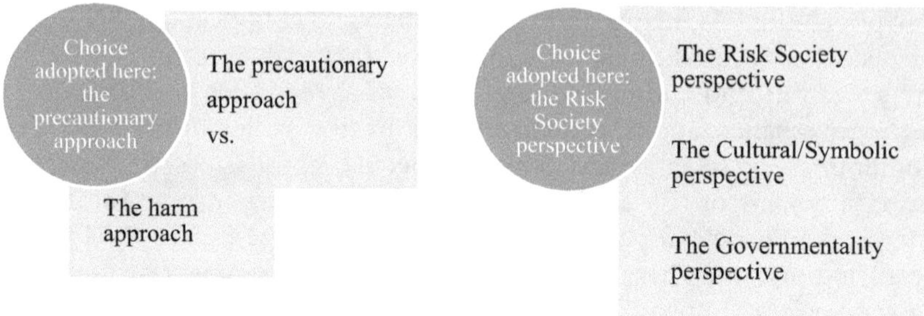

Fig. 2.1 Approaches to the analysis of risk

Risk Categories

The previous paragraphs provided an overview on the controversial nature of the debate on 'risk'. At the end of this section, I will build a working definition of risk to provide a frame for discussion. In order to accomplish this task, I will perform an exercise of categorization: three main definitions of risks from literature on (financial, economic, insurance, information technology and information security, health and safety etc.) risk management and governance are identified here. It should be noted that these definitions are different from the three 'perspectives' discussed above, which instead represent three different sociological interpretations of the notion of risk. However, as the understanding of risk is extremely context-dependent, after analysing the abstract definitions, a series of applied definitions will be discussed.

The first of the three definitions frames risk as an uncertain *event* or condition that, if it occurs, has an effect on at least one protected objective. Here risk is understood as an event or condition that could lead to a harm or to any other undesirable outcome (Project Management Institute 2008). In the second definition, risk is a *number* resulting from the probability of something happening multiplied by the resulting cost or benefit of the happening. This definition understands the risk as a monetary value which is instrumental to quantify and compare levels of risk through the Expected Monetary Value risk impact assessment (Pritchard 2014.) In the third definition, risk is the *probability* or threat resulting in a quantifiable damage, injury, liability, loss, or any other negative outcome caused by a certain happening, which is avoidable through pre-emptive action (Dekker et al. 2004).

From the Oxford English Dictionary, the concept of risk has been broadly defined as a situation involving exposure to danger and as the person or thing regarded as a threat or likely source of danger. These definitions appear closer to the first category, i.e., risk as an event or condition. The Dictionary also defines risk as the possibility that something unwelcome will happen, which instead would be closer to the third definition, i.e., risk as a probability. The Oxford Dictionary provides also two other definitions closer to the second category (i.e., risk as a number/ monetary value) defining risk as the "possibility of harm or damage against which something is insured" or the "possibility of financial loss".[14]

The doctrine has alternatively embraced different understanding of risk. For example, Gellert (2017, 34; 2020) summarizes the concept as "a number-based device, the goal of which is to measure the chance of occurrence of future events (i.e., forecasting) and simultaneously to allow for the taking of decisions on the basis thereof". In this sense, risk would be a number but also a tool for decision-making. The latter understanding of risk would recall what I have discussed *supra* with regard to the regulation of risk 'through risk', and thus the understanding of risk as an *opportunity* for regulation (Power 2007, 28–29).

Risk has been alternatively placed in one of the afore-discussed categories by the literature on risk. For example, it has been framed as an event (first category) by van Asselt and Renn (2011, 437) who define risk as a happening that can entail a *damage* to a recognized material or immaterial good, for example, public health or environmental integrity. Other scholars prefer the third category (risk as a probability) affirming that risk is not the damage itself, because it is not a concrete reality. For example, Rosa (2003, 55) argues that risk is about "certain states of the world which are *possible* (but) not predetermined" [emphasis added].

The debate surrounding risk seems characterized by a series of dichotomies. In the following lines, some of them considered of relevance here are analysed. A first dichotomy is found in Gellert (2017, 34; 2020) with regards to the difference between *risk* and *uncertainty* (see also *infra* in this section). Uncertainties would be "events that unlike risk, cannot be measured through numbers and the formal processes attached thereto. In this sense, risk is quantitative as opposed to uncertainty which is qualitative". Risk would be definable under probabilities (see above the third

[14] Definition by the Oxford English Dictionary, available at https://en.oxforddictionaries.com/definition/risk.

category, i.e., risk as a probability), uncertainty would not. Nevertheless, the authors admits that often the two concepts overlap because risks may be uncertain and "so complex that risk techniques also [have to] include qualitative elements in order to forecast them". Bernstein too seems to blur the boundaries between risk and uncertainty noting that risk exists whenever there is a will to take action in situations that are beyond one's epistemological certainty (Bernstein 1996). In the end, as the notion of risk is essentially an artificial concept (Gellert 2017, 34; 2020), it is foreseeable that there is not objective consensus on whether risk has also traits of uncertainties.

Another dichotomy, to which I already hinted above, is related to risk governance and entails the contraposition between the harm approach and the precautionary approach in handling risks. The first approach justifies action against a certain risk only for certain probabilities of risk and consequential outcomes, as the full array of risks are known or their consequences can be identified and assigned with a probability (Baron 1993). Only scientific certainty would justify the need for action to tackle a specific risk. Differently, the precautionary approach would opt for the prevention of harm to a recognized good, such as health or the environment, despite the scientific uncertainty on whether the harm would occur, rejecting the view that all risks are known and the consequences predictable (Steel 2004).

A third dichotomy, which can create ambiguity, is represented by the circumstance that the same individual can be viewed as *at risk* and, at the same time, as *posing a risk* (Adams and Niezen 2016, 531). From what Adams and Niezen argue (2016, 543), individuals conducting unhealthy lifestyles would be both "at risk of sustaining or resuming bad health habits" and "posing a risk, through their 'unhealthy' behaviour, to the sustainability of the health system and, in turn, to social solidarity". The risk here would be the unhealthy lifestyle—risk as an event—but also the potential diseases and thus health care burden caused by such lifestyle—risk as a probability. Evidently, the discourses surrounding the need to address the 'risk of unhealthy lifestyle' could vary substantially depending on whether one considers those individuals as being *at risk* or *a risk*. From the health domain, this dichotomy could be extended to numerous other fields.[15]

[15] See, for example, present discussions on refugees, who—according to certain opinions—are conceived as risk factors in society but also clearly vulnerable to risks.

Another distinction that has been advanced in the literature and can be understood as dichotomy is between different methods for assessing risks, and mostly two, toxicology and epidemiology. As Demortain illustrated (2011), the first approach would focus on the risk as such (its level) whereas the other would focus upon the consequences of such risk (its effects). I acknowledge that risk management strategies always combine both approaches. Nevertheless, the cases studied in this book align more with the epidemiological understanding of risk and focus on the impact that risk has on individuals.

Lastly, as discussed above, it is worth reflecting on the contraposition between risks that are *external* to human actions and *manufactured* risks (e.g., environmental pollution), which are instead attributable to the modernization process itself. Earlier in this book, I stressed that, whereas in the past the risks were mainly external to human actions, in recent history the second type of risk seems predominant. On those risks, I will focus my attention.

Risk Attributes

A series of adjectives often accompany the word 'risk'. Risks are frequently depicted as 'complex and ambiguous' as they are perceived differently by each affected or concerned stakeholder. This occurs because risk is essentially a social and cultural construction (Johnson and Covello 1987) and it subsists only when people perceive it. Because risks depend on what people value, as illustrated above, various equally legitimate viewpoints exist on whether there is or could be a risk and whether it is tolerable or acceptable. Multiple values creating different and often conflicting perspectives generate ambiguity in risk perception and increase its complexity (van Asselt and Renn 2011, 437). This discussion suggests that risk is a subjective notion and that it may even be impossible to reach a *single* definition of risk. Indeed, numerous sociology scholars stress that the meaning of risk remains *indeterminate* (Beck 2004).

Systemic risks have been characterized as complex (i.e., multi-causal), uncertain and ambiguous (Organization of Economic Cooperation and Development—OECD 2003; Klinke and Renn 2002; Renn 2008). Although often the phrasing 'complex, ambiguous and uncertain risks' is discussed as a whole concept, it seems advisable to unpack these components. Bijker et al. (2009) list four types of risks, drawing on Douglas and Wildavsky (1983): simple, complex, uncertain and ambiguous, and then analyse each of them providing a definition. Rutz et al. (2013, 366), despite presenting each typology in its individuality, add that typologies of risks are often interrelated and can easily shift between categories. Bijker et al. (2009, 159) also support this statement by arguing that "the boundaries between these four risk-problem situations will never be sharp, and they may sometimes even overlap".

A simple risk is defined "in terms of the value of defined outcomes and their relative probability; causes are known and there is an agreement about which interventions are suitable" (Rutz et al. 2013, 365). This category of risk is characterized by certainty both on the cognitive and on the normative aspects of the risk. Simple are those risks that can be described clearly and which occurrence can be calculated statistically. This type of risk can be managed on the basis of "well-established routines" aimed at risk reduction (Bijker et al. 2009, 159). For simple risks, Rutz et al. (2013) seem to embrace the third category of risk, i.e., risk as a probability.

Conversely, in case of complex risks, "it is difficult to determine the cause-effect relationship between a risk agent and its potential consequences" (Rutz et al. 2013, 365; building on OECD 2003; Klinke and Renn 2002; Renn 2008) because the relations between the relevant variables are highly *entangled* (Bijker et al. 2009, 159). This type of risks would be multi-causal as depending on more than few simple factors calculable through statistics. Furthermore, these risks seem highly interrelated with the context in which they are inserted. For complex risks, Rutz et al. adopt the notion of risk as an event, by questioning the link between a cause (the risk agent) and its effect (its potential consequences), rather than its probability.

Uncertain risks instead derive from "situations in which knowledge is incomplete or unavailable" (Rutz et al. 2013, 365; building on OECD 2003; Klinke and Renn 2002; Renn 2008). Consequently, there is a "fundamental scientific uncertainty" over a risk problem (Bijker et al. 2009, 161), despite scientific evidence suggesting that such a risk may be harmful. For this type of risk, a precautionary approach is often advisable and a balance between overprotection and underprotection is to be found, also *in consultation* with the affected stakeholders (Bijker et al. 2009, 161). This typology again suggests an understanding of risk as a probability.

The category of ambiguous risks goes a step further, because it does not only entail "situations in which knowledge is incomplete or unavailable"—as uncertain risks—"but also situations in which the problem cannot be quantified in a reliable manner" and there are "different legitimate viewpoints about what the risk means for those affected" (Rutz et al. 2013, 365; building on OECD 2003; Klinke and Renn 2002; Renn 2008). All the risk situations mentioned so far imply a general agreement on the societal goals and values to be protected. For this latter category, there is instead disagreement on the goals and values themselves, as frequently occurs in pluralistic societies (Bijker et al. 2009, 161). In assessing such risks, the interpretation of knowledge and information, the understanding of what is considered tolerable, and peculiar normative aspects would lead to ambiguity (International Risk Governance Council—IRGC 2005). Ambiguous risks seem concerning a disagreement on the probability of the occurrence of the effect, given the presentation of the event, which would suggest a focus on the third category, i.e., risk as a probability.

In addition, another relevant attribute is that of 'systemic' risks. Simple risks are opposed to systemic risks. Systemic risks would be the combination of complexity (multiple causes) and uncertainty. Moreover, they would be highly embedded in those societal contexts and processes that cause such risks (OECD 2003). The magnitude and impact of systemic risk are particularly elevated. For example, in the financial sector, systemic risks have been defined as the risk of collapse of an entire financial system or an entire market. Another dichotomy emerges here, i.e., between the described systemic risks and idiosyncratic risks, the second type affecting only a single institution or asset without rippling out into the rest of the system.[16]

I acknowledge the existence of numerous other categorizations in the literature. For example, Wynne (1992) distinguishes between risk, uncertainty, ignorance and indeterminacy, and von Schomberg (2006) distinguishes between risk, unquantifiable risk, epistemic uncertainty and hypothetical effect. The impossibility to cover all these nuances makes the present review only a non-exhaustive illustration of selected approaches to risk characterization from the literature. Yet, sketching these typologies has an important role here. As I will note discussing Bijker et al. (2009),

[16] See http://www.systemicrisk.ac.uk/.

I consider certain types of risks more 'apt' to be dealt with through citizen sensing. In other words, I regard citizen sensing as particularly beneficial in situations of *conflict* over a risk problem. These conflictive scenarios are often found in relation to uncertain and ambiguous risks. Bijker et al. (2009, 162, 164) stress that, participatory process involving the citizens in risk governance are needed exclusively for these types of risk. According to the authors, for simple risks traditional institutional governance would be preferable. I support the view valuing citizens' input especially in case of uncertain and ambiguous risk problems. However, I think that citizen sensing could be beneficial also in case of simpler risk scenarios.

The Importance of Risk Perception

Risk perception and risk governance strategies that account for this dimension are fundamental elements of this research. Claims against a 'black box' risk governance, unaccountable and obscure, are often associated with a lack of consideration of how concerned actors perceive the risk. The book "Risk Communication for the Future" edited by Bourrier and Bieder (2018) provides an extensive accounting of the 'perceptional' dimension of risk, inspecting a wide range of situations where risk and public communication were at stake. In the book, headings span from "Nuclear Crisis Preparedness [and] Lessons Learned from Fukushima Daiichi" to "The Collapse of Absolute Trust in Absolute Truth". From the study of Bourrier and Bieder (2018), personal factors emerge as crucial element that matter in risk communication perception and reaction. In addition, people's risk perception is said to often increase after some years from an accident because they realized the 'real impact' of the risk. Time thus also matters for risk perception. In spite of the acknowledged importance of time and of history in understanding risk perception, there are inherent limits to people and institutions' ability to learn from experience in case of low probability high-consequences events, while a short-term forgetting effect is dominant. Communication with and to affected stakeholders, *trust* in the process, consideration of time and learning from past events result in being important factors to shape risk perception(s).

In a discussion on the lessons to be learnt for (radiological) risk communication from the COVID-19 pandemic held in March 2020,[17] the shortcomings of risk communication to the public were outlined. The discussants stressed the collective inability to learn from past experience and the problem of different communication approaches in different countries and cultural contexts, as well as conflicting expert/policy opinions often generating even more uncertainty and distrust from the people. It was timely noted that the more the information is uncertain, the better communication should be Lastly, it was noted that, despite all communication efforts, policy-makers would have been confronted with the doubt on whether citizens would follow their indications and *trust* them.

Another element crucial to risk perception is that of culture, as embedded in lay knowledge. Stressing the connection between cultural legacy, health and lay knowledge, Haklay launched a quite assertive post on his blog titled “Indigenous People on the Front Lines: Using Citizen Science to Improve Environmental Public Health”,[18] inspired by a session held at the Citizen Science Conference 2019. Haklay voices the stories of successful inclusion of indigenous knowledge through citizen science in risk response strategies. Subjective risk perception and lay knowledge on the risk, despite not always fully reflecting the reality, can be precious for orienting risk governance. Subjective perception of air pollution, for example, can be essential for designing cleaner-air policies. A study, conducted under the EU-funded “Physical Activity through Sustainable Transport Approaches—PASTA” project, has analysed the link between level of concern over health effects of air pollution and personal and environmental factors in seven European cities. Overall, 58% of participants were worried over health effects of air pollution, with large differences between cities. On a city scale, average levels of concern over health effects of air pollution had a good correlation with average NO2 levels and a lower correlation with average PM2.5 levels (Dons et al. 2018). This showed that, in some instances, risk perception and reality match.

[17] SHARE Webinar: “Lessons we are learning from the COVID-19 pandemic for radiological risk communication”, March 16, 2020. See https://www.ssh-share.eu/webinar/.

[18] See https://povesham.wordpress.com/2019/03/16/citizen-science-2019-indigenous-people-on-the-front-lines-using-citizen-science-to-improve-environmental-public-health/.

The relevance of risk perception for risk governance has stimulated the development of tools such as the Social Amplification of Risk Framework (SARF). Proposed first by Kasperson et al. (1988), SARF is a theoretical tool for understanding how risks are perceived, interpreted and amplified or attenuated in the way they are communicated throughout an identified society. The tool is useful to inspect the interplay between official risk communication, media coverage and individual and social perception of the risk. In some of the cases discussed in this research, the element of 'social amplification' will result in being crucial. Amplification of risk perception can be associated with the feeling of being misled or not properly informed by the authorities competent for handling the risk. The discussion on risk perception and on the role of the feeling to 'be misled' on an actual risk is exemplified by the Sandman formula (Sandman 1993) according to which the higher the sense of outrage, the stronger people will perceive risk. The situation surrounding a risk, the type of risk and how this is managed may trigger outrage. Arguably, transparency, engagement of the affected people in risk handling and access to the decision-making processes could reduce the sense of outrage in communities and individuals affected by risks (Sandman 1993). Notorious cases are those of the tobacco and sugar production lobbies purposely hiding to the public the real health hazards associated with their products or the gas and oil industry denying climate science. In all these instances, risk perception was seriously affected by perceiving to be in the hands of 'black box' science and policy-making (Taubes 2017).

Authors have noted that, especially when these types of feelings spread, individuals often turn to the Internet for a resort, both to find easily accessible contents produced by peer laypersons and to access experts' resources to find different interpretation of the risk (Stasik and Jemielniak 2021). This may produce the effect of having people contest institutional science, because of its lack of transparency; in other cases, laypersons use expert knowledge produced and available on different platforms to challenge the dominant risk governance approaches, for example, bringing global discussions to specific locations (Stasik and Jemielniak 2021). In doing so, citizens increasingly become 'scientifically literate' (achieving a sort of 'scientific citizenship') which is essential in order to be engaged in science and policy-making (Ellis and Waterton 2004). This in certain fields is almost a prerequisite of participation, considering the increasing 'scientification' of policies (Ellis and Waterton 2004). However, for the illustrated importance played by risk perception, there seems to be the need that also scientists and policy-makers become 'societally literate', i.e., their reasoning should also reflect social dimensions such as risk perception. In the end, citizens' input can properly be integrated in risk policy-making only if scientists and policy-makers *also* take the perspective of the citizens.

Overall, and considering the preceding reflections, it can be argued that the importance of risk perception pervades the definition of risk. The epistemological understanding of risk is indeed heavily influenced by risk perception-related aspects, which—in turn—depends on factors external to the risk such as gender, target, value system and how risks are communicated. Renn and Klinke thoroughly inspected the issue of different risk perceptions specifically in relation to environmental risk governance strategies (Renn and Klinke 2016), providing a critical perspective. The authors indeed argue (Renn and Klinke 2016, 1) that it is necessary to consider "the major psychological and social mechanisms of [risk] perception" because "false information or perception biases" could undermine the validity of the laypersons' knowledge over risks. The different viewpoints on risk and risk perceptions make it difficult to agree on a standard definition of risk. There would be contextual factors not definable a priori that heavily shape how risk is configured and perceived. In analysing the factors particularly influential for the policy uptake of citizen sensing, I stress the importance of accounting for citizens' perception biases in the measurements to be credible in the eyes of fellow citizens and institutions.

All this discussion on the importance of risk perceptions and its nuances conflicts with attempts to (over-)simplify the concept of risk. An example of these simplification efforts are the reflections of the economist Knight (1921), who argued that risk—in contrast to uncertainty—covers situations where we do not know the consequences of a certain danger, but these can be *accurately calculated* (e.g., through statistics). Uncertainty would instead refer to those situations where the information necessary to calculate the odds is missing. This can be true for simple and unambiguous risks. However, as most of the risks of today's society do not fall under this category, I argue that risk governors should pay attention to contextual factors such as risk perception. As stressed by van Asselt and Renn (2011, 436), the calculation of risks as a linear function of probability and cause-effects chain cannot cope with complex, uncertain and ambiguous risks. This need for an in-depth analysis of risks

Fig. 2.2 From uncertain, ambiguous and complex problems to citizen sensing

calls for increasingly sophisticated and inclusive approaches to risk governance. My research aims to contribute to this debate adding a piece of the puzzle, i.e., the citizen sensing approach to risk governance, as illustrated in Fig. 2.2.

Definitions of Risk in Practice

The abstract categories previously discussed have been applied to specific contexts, where different bodies chose to adopt one definition of risk rather than another. In this sub-section, I will connect selected institutional definitions with the three categories of risk discussed above.

In the daily practice of risk governance, risk has been recognized as an all-comprehensive word that represents *a variety of situations*. As the Health Council of the Netherlands points out (1995), "not all risks are equal". Risks differ considerably in terms of probability and effects, dose and response, causes and factors, agent and consequences, type and magnitude, time of occurrence as and duration, possibilities of recovery etc. (Berti Suman 2018a). Organizations have developed tools to categorize the complexity and variety of risks. In the political arena, the German Advisory Council on Global Change (WBGU 2000; Klinke and Renn 2011; Renn, Klinke and van Asselt 2011) introduced criteria, such as the 'incertitude' variable linked to the uncertainty in knowledge, to be considered when modelling complex systems or predicting a risk. Another important criterion is that of 'ubiquity', i.e., geographical dispersion of possible damages, which is particularly relevant to this study because ubiquitous risks activate distant actors and communities that respond through *networks* (for example, citizen sensing networks). Lastly, the criterion of the 'potential for mobilization', is considered relevant as it resonates with the here central concept of 'social uptake'. For mobilization, however, the Council refers to the broad social impact and potential social conflict that the risk will generate. Social conflict and clashes between visions in situation of information unbalances will be analysed as triggers for citizen sensing.

In the political arena and with regards to the health domain, the Health Council of the Netherlands, the Health Council of the Netherlands (1995) defines 'risk' as "the possibility, with a certain degree of probability, of damage to health, environment and goods, in combination with the nature and magnitude of the damage". The causes of risk, according to the opinion of the Council, are action by man, natural events or combinations of these. The definition privileges the third understanding of risk, i.e., risk as a probability, and put particular emphasis on damage to health and damage to the environment (Berti Suman 2018b), which is particularly relevant for this research. Another political body, the IRGC (2005, 20), stated that "risk refers to tolerated or unintended consequences of purposeful human actions which may occur that violate something that humans *value*" [emphasis added]. In this sense, risk would entail a qualitative judgement of value, definition which may be closer to the second category of risk, i.e., risk as a number or a monetary value (although, risk as a number also suggests a quantitative assessment).

With regards to the more specific notion of 'environmental risk to public health', the WHO[19] defines a risk factor to public health as "any attribute, characteristic or exposure of an individual that increases the likelihood of developing a disease or injury". In this sense, the WHO embraces the first understanding of risk, i.e., risk as an event or condition. Some examples of the most important risk factors according to the WHO's definition are "[...] high blood pressure, tobacco and alcohol consumption, and unsafe water, sanitation and hygiene." In the twenty-first century, and in particular in developed countries, the main risks posed by environmental factors to public health are connected to environmental contaminants and climate change (Berti Suman 2018a; WHO[20]). The WHO wording seems again failing to include those socio-cultural aspects and psychosocial risk factors illustrated above. Still from a political body in the health domain, risk is defined as "the combination of the probability of a hazard resulting in an adverse event, and the severity of the event"

[19] See the WHO website: http://www.who.int/topics/risk_factors/en/.

[20] See the WHO website: http://www.euro.who.int/en/health-topics/Health-systems/public-health-services/public-health-services.

by the Occupational Health & Safety Advisory Services (OHSAS), issuing the Certification 18,001:2007.[21] This definition includes elements of all three categorizations of risk.

A Working Definition of Risk

The preceding discussion has been functional to reach a working definition of 'environmental risk to public health'. This research adopts the first understanding of risk, considering environmental health risk as "an uncertain event (e.g., a radiation leak) or phenomenon (e.g., noise) that is likely to affect public health, while there may be scientific uncertainty/ disagreement on whether the consequences of this event will be harmful for public health". Uncertainty and disagreement suggest that it is a matter of complex, uncertain and/or ambiguous risks and that a precautionary approach should be adopted. Furthermore, most of the risks at issue in this research are manufactured risks, entailing a high degree of human agency (for example, air pollution deriving from urban congestion). As the individual can be viewed as both the agent causing the risk (risk agent) and one of the subjects exposed to the risk (in addition to other affected forms of life, for those citizen sensing projects tackling also loss of environmental resources and biodiversity), the dichotomy 'at risk' versus 'posing a risk' applies here. Citizen sensing is consequently regarded as a set of tools/practices aimed at, first, assessing the event/ phenomenon and, secondly, at measuring whether there is a causal link between an event/phenomenon (radiation, noise) and an effect (harm for public health). The working definition of environmental risk to public health is illustrated in Fig. 2.3.

Governance and Risk Governance

This section elaborates the notion of 'risk governance' starting from the discussion of the 'governance' component. The notion of *governance* primarily belongs to the political sciences and aims at describing "the multitude of actors and processes that lead to collective binding decisions" (van Asselt and Renn 2011, 431). The term governance captures

[21] See OHSAS 18001:2007 "Occupational Health and Safety Management Certification", available at https://www.certificationeurope.com/app/uploads/2017/12/OHSAS-18001.pdf.

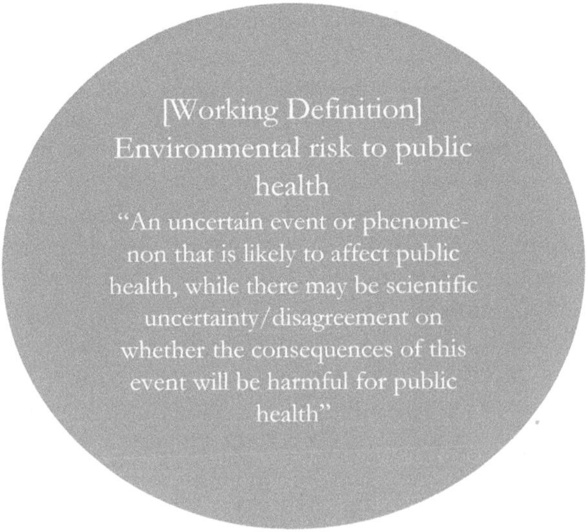

Fig. 2.3 A working definition of environmental risk to public health

the interplay between governmental institutions, economic forces and—particularly relevant for this study—civil society actors. Governance (as a 'phenomenon') takes place within this ***horizontally organized*** structure encompassing both state and non-state actors (including citizens) interacting among themselves (Wolf 2002). While the term 'government' evokes a vertical structure, the term 'governance' goes beyond the state-focus to embrace the breadth and complexity of the numerous interactions occurring horizontally among several actors shaping the socio-political scene. The need to devote attention to this ***multitude of actors*** competing with the government and organized in ***multi-actor networks*** is the main message of the focus shift from 'government' to 'governance'. Within this book, the governance perspective assumes a specific meaning for the role reserved to citizen engagement in this new political setting. The citizen sensing practices studied here are inserted in a 'governance momentum' in today's political scenarios, which can be dated back to the 1980s. If the governance turn originated in the domain of development studies, it has gradually pervaded other domains of the political discourse, from international relations to environmental and health studies, risk research, and—timely—the citizen science/sensing discourses.

As van Asselt and Renn point out (2011, 435), the word 'governance' has both a descriptive and a normative meaning. As a descriptive notion, it refers to the "*complex web* of manifold interactions between *heterogeneous actors*" [emphasis added] which describes the current state of political processes and structures (van Asselt and Renn 2011, 435). In a normative sense, it illustrates an emerging "model or framework for organizing and managing society" (van Asselt and Renn 2011, 435). The European Commission, in the 2001 White Paper on Governance, adopts the normative view by presenting governance as an alternative model to more top-down forms of governing, in which "transparency, *stakeholder participation*, *accountability*, and policy coherence are key principles" [emphasis added]. This research aligns with a normative understanding of governance, as promoting participation and accountability in (risk) decision-making. Moreover, the lens adopted here also aims at reversing this perspective, considering participation itself as a value for good governance and as an alternative to 'top-down' decision-making.

Moving attention to the notion of 'risk governance', relevant authors in the field (among which van Asselt and Renn 2011; Amendola 2001; Elliott 2001) argued that this relatively recent concept originated from European research networks spanning various domains, from sociological and psychological research on risk, to Science and Technology Studies (STS), political sciences and legal doctrine (van Asselt and Renn 2011, 432). The breadth of the relevant scholarship demonstrates the complexity of the topic and the perceived need to address it from different angles, both theoretically and empirically. This research is built on this ongoing debate on risk governance, but privileges the socio-legal aspects of it and focuses on the specific application of citizen sensing to risk governance.

Van Asselt and Renn (2011, 431) framed risk governance as "the translation of the substance and core principles of governance to the context of risk-related decision-making", as illustrated in Fig. 2.4. Risk governance thus includes "both the institutional structure and the policy process that guide and restrain collective activities of a group, society or international community to regulate, reduce or control risk problems" (Renn, Klinke and Van Asselt 2011, 231). As I noted in Berti Suman 2018a, the debate on governance shaped the discussion on *risk* governance. This means that when the notion of risk governance arose, it was already influenced by the discussion on the transition from 'government' to 'governance'. The *government* of the risk is thus not discussed, but rather its *governance* (Berti Suman 2018a), thus including the above-mentioned "complex web of manifold interactions between heterogeneous actors" (van Asselt and Renn 2011, 435). Yet, the analysis developed in this book clearly has implications also for government of the risk and for risk governors, especially for what concerns the conceivable obligations for the State to listen to the sensing citizens resulting from my analysis.

As illustrated above for the concept of governance, also risk governance can have a descriptive and a normative meaning. In the descriptive sense, it would be "the critical study of complex, interacting networks in which choices and decisions are made around risks" (van Asselt and Renn 2011, 443). The mention of these 'complex, interacting networks' stresses that risks, in the sense adopted in this research,[22] are governed not only through the intervention of formal institutions and procedures, but also through 'informal arrangements' (van Asselt and Renn 2011, 432). The informality element is particularly relevant for this research because the grassroots sensing practices discussed exactly originate in informal settings where lay actors take the lead. The grassroots-driven production of knowledge, the gaining of legitimacy and the subsequent formal

Fig. 2.4 Risk governance at the intersection of the debate on risk and on governance

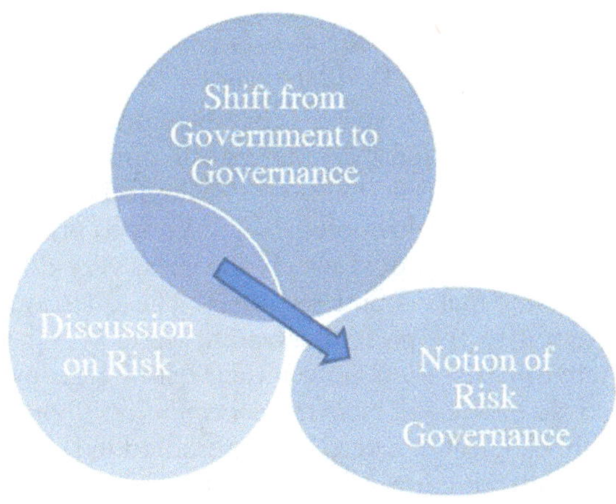

[22] Risks are defined in this project as uncertain events (e.g., a radiation leak) or phenomena (e.g., noise) that are likely to affect public health, see discussion *supra*.

recognition of these informal practices (Berti Suman 2018a) will be investigated, constantly in confrontation with what simultaneously happens at the institutional level.

In the normative sense, risk governance would represent "a set of normative principles which can inform *all relevant actors of society* on how to deal *responsibly* with risks" [emphasis added] (van Asselt and Renn 2011, 443). According to this second definition, risk governance would provide a normative basis for orienting decision-making, especially, on uncertain, complex and ambiguous risks (van Asselt and Renn 2011, 432). The normative definition recalls the aims of my research for the attention it puts on a responsible governance of the risk and for the inclusion of all relevant actors of society (thus including also members of the civil society such as the sensing citizens). I here embrace Renn, Klinke and van Asselt's argument (2011, 1) that, in spite of the possible fragmentation of multi-actors participatory models of risk governance, institutional diversity brings the promise to actually improve the governance of the risk and contribute to societal resiliency. In such models, non-state actors play a crucial role as holders of decisive advantages of information and resources, which are unavailable to institutional actors (Kern and Bulkeley 2009). Consequently, the key question is how to better make use of these informational advantages and resources to enhance risk governance.

Case Insight. 1: Public and Environmental Health Risk Governance in the Chernobyl Disaster

An outstanding analysis of the concepts discussed in the preceding sections has been provided by the anthropologist Petryna (2013) in her book titled "Life Exposed. Biological Citizens after Chernobyl". The author used anthropological methods to provide an account of social realities after Chernobyl which appear as very different from those described by policy-makers and scientists. The questions driving her inquiry, very relevant to the present research, were: "[W]hat happens to politics when state officials *fail to inform* their fellow citizens of real threats to life? What are *the moral and political consequences of remedies* available in the wake of technological disasters?" [emphasis added]. Interestingly, Petryna wrote a new introduction in 2013, adding to the 2003's version also reflections on the Fukushima disaster, which she reads in comparison to Chernobyl.

For reasons of focus, only few aspects of Petryna's study are discussed here. A first element that I wish to take from Petryna's anthropological investigation is the way the people that lived Chernobyl achieved a "domestication" of an "overwhelming risk" (Petryna 2013, xvii). A push to a new sort of normality and a nearly opportunistic approach to the fact of "being a victim"—and thus claiming such a "biological citizenship"—emerges (Petryna 2013, xvii). The idea of domestication of the risk, i.e., the risk becomes part of people's daily life, recalls what I argued here in relation to the development of a *unique knowledge* over a risk problem through facing it daily. A biological citizenship describes the individual and collective welfare claims made by populations that were biologically damaged for having been exposed to the nuclear disaster. Such claims recall what I have discussed here in terms of demands to an accountable governance of the risk. In Petryna (2013), however, these claims are depicted as almost opportunistic as the citizens at instances abuse the fact of having suffered from the effect of the disaster to get financial redress and other benefits from the state and not really to seek justice.

Petryna, in line with some of the arguments developed here, criticizes a debate on the future of nuclear power which is "based not on emotions but on arguments and facts" (Petryna 2013, xix) or, in other words, what the author calls "a nonpeopled approach" (Petryna 2013, xx). I will argue that both facts and emotions are crucial and that ways to make emotions (and risk perceptions) matter for risk governance is of utmost importance, especially when the lived experience of the disaster clashes with what scientists and policy documents tell.

Timely, Petryna refers to Fukushima, noting that, after the 2011 nuclear catastrophe, "citizens worldwide require a reliable measure of the human consequences of chronic exposure to low-dose radiation from nuclear accidents" (Petryna 2013, xxi). The author argues that Chernobyl could have provided that measure, but failed to do so, which seems to recall an argument developed here on the criticisms of a reactive rather than preventive risk governance. Chernobyl and Fukushima align in some aspects, for example, the ideal—dominant in the disaster's aftermath—that the State is in control, vanishing soon after, when disorientation and injury spread. Nonetheless, Petryna argues that Fukushima "illustrates that there is more than one way to have Chernobyl" (Petryna 2013, xxiv). The author mostly refers to the different cases that led to the two disasters and their different dynamics of developments, Yet, I wonder if Petryna also implicitly refers to the fact that the two disasters took place under very different states and historical contexts. Further connections between Chernobyl and Fukushima's disasters have been discussed in the work of Abe (2020) in a study on how post-Fukushima civic measurement practices were influenced by earlier experiences that developed after Chernobyl.

Lastly, a statement from the anthropologist that condenses this book's reflections on the tensions between experts, lay knowledge and power is the following: "The processes of making scientific knowledge are inextricable from the forms of power those processes legitimate and even provide solutions for" (Petryna 2013, 10).

References

Abe, Y. 2020. "Citizen before Science: R-DAN and its monitorial ethic after Chernobyl." In *Legal, social and ethical perspectives on health & technology*, ed. Fathisalout-Bollon, M. and A. Berti Suman. Paris: Lextenso Editions.

Acheson, D. 1988. *Public health in England: The report of the committee of inquiry into the future development of the public health function.* London: HMSO.

Adamkiewicz, G., et al. 2011. "Moving environmental justice indoors: Understanding structural influences on residential exposure patterns in low-income communities." *American Journal of Public Health* 101 (S1): 238–245.

Adams, S.A. and M. Niezen. 2016. "Digital 'solutions' to unhealthy lifestyle 'problems': The construction of social and personal risks in the development of eCoaches." *Health Risk & Society* 17 (7–8): 530–546. https://doi.org/10.1080/13698575.2015.1136409.

Amendola, A. 2001. "Recent paradigms for risk informed decision making." *Safety Science* 40 (1–4): 17–30.

Baron, J. 1993. *Morality and rational choice.* Dordrecht: Springer, Science+Business Media.

Bates, D.V. 1994. *Environmental health risks and public policy. Decision making in free societies*. Seattle and London: University of Washington Press.

Beck, U. 1992. *Risk society: Towards a new modernity*. London: Sage Publications.

Beck, U. 2004. *A critical introduction to the risk society*. London: Pluto Press.

Beck, U. 2015. "Emancipatory catastrophism: What does it mean to climate change and risk society?" *Current Sociology* 63 (1): 75–88. https://doi.org/10.1177/0011392114559951.

Bernstein, P.L. 1996. *Against the gods—The remarkable story of risk.* New York: John Wiley & Sons.

Berti Suman, A. 2018a. "Challenging risk governance patterns through citizen sensing: The Schiphol Airport case". International Review of

Law, Computers & Technology 32(1). https://doi.org/10.1080/13600869.2018.1429186.

Berti Suman, A. 2018b. "The smart transition: An opportunity for a sensor-based public-health risk governance?" *International Review of Law, Computers & Technology* 32 (2–3), Special issue on 'Smart Cities or Smart Machines: Data Infrastructures and the Rule(s) of Law': 257–274. https://doi.org/10.1080/13600869.2018.1463961.

Bijker, W.E., R. Bal and R. Hendriks. 2009. *The paradox of scientific authority: The role of scientific advice in democracies*. Cambridge, MA: The MIT Press.

Bourrier, M. and C. Bieder. 2018. *Risk communication for the future. Towards smart risk governance and safety management*. SpringerBriefs in Applied Sciences and Technology. Heidelberg: Springer.

Briggs, D.J. 2008. "A framework for integrated environmental health impact assessment of systemic risks." *Environmental Health* 7 (1): 61.

Cecez-Kecmanovic, D. and M. Janson. 1999. "Communicative action theory: An approach to understanding the application of information systems." *Proceedings of the 10th Australasian Conference on Information Systems ACISí99*, Wellington, New Zealand: 183–195.

Dalbokova, D. and M. Krzyzanowski. 2002. "Environmental health indicators: Development of a methodology for the WHO European Region." *Statistical Journal of the United Nations Economic Commission for Europe* 19 (1, 2): 93–103.

Dekker, M., D.A. Hillson and D.T. Hulett. 2004. "Assessing risk probability: Alternative approaches." *Proceedings of PMI Global Congress 2004*, Prague, Czech Republic.

Demortain, D. 2011. *Scientists and the regulation of risk—Standardising control*. Cheltenham, UK: Edward Elgar.

Dickinson, A.D. and K.E. Iles. 2017. "Environmental health: Overview." In *International encyclopedia of public health*, 2nd ed., 487–498. https://doi.org/10.1016/B978-0-12-803678-5.00133-8.

Dons, E., et al. 2018. "Concern over health effects of air pollution is associated to NO2 in seven European cities." *Air Quality, Atmosphere & Health* 11 (5): 591–599. https://doi.org/10.1007/s11869-018-0567-3.

Douglas, M. 1970. *Natural symbols: Explorations in cosmology*. London: Barrie & Jenkins Press.

Douglas, M. 1992. *Risk and blame: Essays in cultural theory*. London: Routledge.

Douglas, M. and A. Wildavsky. 1983. *Risk and culture. An essay on the selection of technological and environmental dangers*. Berkeley, CA: University of California Press.

Elliott, D. 2001. "Risk governance: Is consensus a con?" *Science as Culture* 10 (2): 265–271.

Ellis, R. and C. Waterton. 2004. "Environmental citizenship in the making: The participation of volunteer naturalists in UK biological recording and biodiversity policy." *Science and Public Policy* 31 (2): 95–105. https://doi.org/10.3152/147154304781780055.

Foucault, M. 1991. "Governmentality." In Burchell, G., C. Gordon and P. Miller (eds.) *The Foucault effect: Studies in governmentality*, 87–104. Chicago, IL: University of Chicago Press.

Foucault, Michel. 1979 (original language 1976). *The history of sexuality volume 1: An introduction*. London: Allen Lane.

Frank, L.D. and P.O. Engelke. 2001. "The built environment and human activity patterns: Exploring the impacts of urban form on public health." *CPL bibliography* 16 (2): 202–218.

Gee, G.C. and D. Payne-Sturges. 2004. "Environmental health disparities: A framework integrating psychosocial and environmental concepts." *Environmental health perspectives* 112 (17).

Gellert, R. 2015. "Data protection: A risk regulation? Between the risk management of everything and the precautionary alternative." *International Data Privacy Law* 5 (1): 3–19.

Gellert, R. 2017. *Understanding the risk-based approach to data protection: An analysis of the links between law, regulation, and risk.* Dissertation defended at the Vrije Universiteit Brussel. Published as Gellert, R. 2020. *The risk-based approach to data protection.* Oxford: Oxford University Press.

Georgiadou, P. Y., J. H. Lungo and C. Richter. 2014. "Citizen sensors or extreme publics? Transparency and accountability interventions on the mobile geoweb". *International journal of digital earth* 7(7): 516–533. https://doi.org/10.1080/17538947.2013.782073.

Giddens, A. 1990. *The consequences of modernity*. Cambridge, UK: Polity Press.

Giddens, A. 1998. *The third way: The renewal of social democracy*. Cambridge, UK: Polity Press.

Gieryn, T.F. 1983. "Boundary-work and the demarcation of science from non-science: Strains and interests in professional ideologies of scientists." *American Sociological Review* 48: 781–795.

Gieryn, T.F. 1999. *Cultural boundaries of science: Credibility on the line*. Chicago: University of Chicago Press.

Gostin, L.O. 2000. *Public health regulation: A systematic evaluation, public law and legal theory.* Working Paper No. 242584, Georgetown University Law Center.

Habermas, J. 1984. *The theory of communicative action—Reason and rationalization of society*, Vol. 1. Boston: Beacon Press.

Haines, A., R.S. Kovats, D. Campbell-Lendrum and C. Corvalán. 2006. "Climate change and human health: Impacts, vulnerability and public health." *Public health* 120 (7): 585–596.

Health Council of the Netherlands. 1995. Not All Risks Are Equal. Report No. 1995 06E, Committee on Risk Measures and Risk Assessment, Hague.

Hobsbawm, E.J. 1969. *Industry and empire. From 1750 to the present day*. London: Penguin Books.

International Risk Governance Council—IRGC. 2005. *Risk governance: Towards an integrative approach*. White Paper No. 1 by Renn, O., with Annex by Graham, P. Geneva: IRGC.

Irwin, A. 1995. *Citizen science: A study of people, expertise and sustainable development*. London: Routledge.

Jackson, T. 1996. *Material concerns: Pollution, profit and quality of life*. London: Routledge.

Johnson, B. and V. Covello. 1987. "The social and cultural construction of risk. Essays on risk selection and perception." *Technology, Risk, and Society* 3. https://doi.org/10.1007/978-94-009-3395-8.

Kasperson, R.E., et al. 1988. "The social amplification of risk: A conceptual framework." *Risk Analysis*, 8: 177–187. https://doi.org/10.1111/j.1539-6924.1988.tb01168.x.

Kern, K. and H. Bulkeley. 2009. "Cities, Europeanization and multilevel governance: Governing climate change through transnational municipal networks." *Journal of Common Market Studies* 3: 309–332.

Klinke, A. and O. Renn. 2002. "A new approach to risk evaluation and management: Risk-based, precaution-based and discourse-based management." *Risk Analysis* 22 (6): 1071–1094. https://doi.org/10.1111/1539-6924.00274.

Klinke, A. and O. Renn. 2011. "Adaptive and integrative governance on risk and uncertainty." *Journal of Risk Research* 15 (3): 273–292. https://doi.org/10.1080/13669877.2011.636838.

Knight, F.H. 1921. *Risk, uncertainty, and profit*. Boston, MA: Houghton Mifflin.

Laakkonen, S., R.P. Tucker and T. Vuorisalo. 2017. *The long shadows. A global environmental history of the second world war*. Corvallis: Oregon State University Press.

Lebret, E. 2016. "Integrated environmental health impact assessment for risk governance purposes; Across what do we integrate?" *International Journal of Environmental Research and Public Health* 13 (1): 71. https://doi.org/10.3390/ijerph13010071.

Lupton, D. 1993. "Risk as moral danger: The social and political functions of risk discourse in public health." *International Journal of Health Services* 23 (3): 425–435. https://doi.org/10.2190/16AYE2GC-DFLD-51X2.

Lupton, D. 2015. "Health promotion in the digital era: A critical commentary." *Health Promotion International* 30 (1): 174–183. https://doi.org/10.1093/heapro/dau091.

Oliver, T. R. 2006. "The politics of public health policy." *Annual Review of Public Health* 27: 195–233.

Organization of Economic Cooperation and Development—OECD. 2003. *Emerging systemic risks*. Final Report to the OECD Futures Project. Paris: OECD.

Pellow, D.N., A. Weinberg and A. Schnaiberg. 2001. "The environmental justice movement: Equitable allocation of the costs and benefits of environmental management outcomes." *Social Justice Research* 14 (4): 423–439.

Petryna, A. 2013. *Life exposed: Biological citizens after Chernobyl*. Princeton: Princeton University Press.

Pickett, B.L. 1995. "Foucault and the politics of resistance." *Polity* 28 (4): 445–466.

Polzer, J. and E. Power. 2016. *Neoliberal governance and health: Duties, risks, vulnerability*. Montreal: McGill-Queen's University Press.

Power, M. 2007. *Organized uncertainty: Designing a world of risk management*. Oxford: Oxford University Press.

Pritchard, L.C. 2014. "Decision analysis: Expected monetary value." In *Risk management concepts and guidance*, ed. Pritchard, L.C., 5th ed., 207–217. Auerbach Publications: New York.

Project Management Institute. 2008. *A guide to the project management body of knowledge*. Newtown Square, PA: Project Management Institute.

Pyysiäinen, J., D. Halpin and A. Guilfoyle. 2017. "Neoliberal governance and 'responsibilization' of agents: Reassessing the mechanisms of responsibility-shift in neoliberal discursive environments." *Distinktion: Journal of Social Theory* 18 (2): 215–235. https://doi.org/10.1080/1600910X.2017.1331858.

Quelle, C. Unpublished. *The normative side of risk management in the area of data protection*. Working paper.

Renn, O. 2008. *Risk governance: Coping with uncertainty in a complex world*. London: Earthscan.

Renn, O. and A. Klinke. 2016. "Risk perception and its impacts on risk governance." In *Oxford research encyclopedia of environmental science*. Oxford: Oxford University Press. https://doi.org/10.1093/acrefore/9780199389414.013.2.

Renn, O., Klinke, A. and M. van Asselt. 2011. "Coping with complexity, uncertainty and ambiguity in risk governance: A synthesis." *AMBIO* 40: 231–246. https://doi.org/10.1007/s13280-010-0134-0.

Ricci, P. 2006. *Environmental and health risk assessment and management. Principles and practices*. Dordrecht: Springer.

Rosa, E.A. 2003. "The logical structure of the social amplification of risk framework (SARF): Metatheoretical foundations and policy implications." In *The social amplification of risk*, ed. Pidgeon, N., Kasperson, R.E. and P. Slovic, 47–79. Cambridge: Cambridge University Press.

Rosa, E.A., O. Renn and A.M. McCright. 2013. *The risk society revisited: Social theory and governance*. Philadelphia: Temple University Press.

Rose, G. 1989. "Science, ethics and public policy." In *Assessment of health hazards*, ed. Mohr, U. Heidelberg and New York: Springer Verlag.

Rose, N. 1992. "Governing the enterprising self". In Heelas, P. and P. Morris (Eds.) *The values of the enterprise culture: The moral debate*. London: Routledge, pp. 141–164.

Rose, N., P. O'Malley and M. Valverde. 2006. "Governmentality." *Annual Review of Law and Social Science* 2: 83–104. https://doi.org/10.1146/annurev.lawsocsci.2.081805.105900.

Rutz, S.I., S.A. Adams, S.E. Buitendijk, P.B.M. Robben and A.A. de Bont. 2013. "Hiding complexity, uncertainty and ambiguity: How inspectorates simplify issues to create enforceable action." *Health, Risk & Society* 15 (4): 363–379. https://doi.org/10.1080/13698575.2013.796343.

Sandman, P.M. 1993. *Responding to community outrage: Strategies for effective risk communication*. Fairfax, VA: American Industrial Hygiene Association.

Santoriello, G. 2019. *Colonia Basilicata*. COVA Contro.

Spruijt, P., A.B. Knol, E. Vasileiadou, J. Devilee, E. Lebret and A.C. Petersen. 2014. "Roles of scientists as policy advisers on complex issues: A literature review." *Environmental Science & Policy* 40: 16–25. https://doi.org/10.1016/j.envsci.2014.03.002.

Srinivasan, S., L.R. O'Fallon and A. Dearry. 2003. "Creating healthy communities, healthy homes, healthy people: Initiating a research agenda on the built environment and public health." *American Journal of Public Health* 93 (9): 1446–1450.

Star, S.L. and J.R. Griesemar. 1989. "Institutional ecology, 'translations,' and boundary objects: Amateurs and professionals in Berkeley's Museum of Vertebrate Zoology, 1907-1939." *Social Studies of Science* 19: 387–420.

Stasik, A. and D. Jemielniak. 2021. "Public involvement in risk governance in the internet era: Impact of new rules of building trust and credibility." *Journal of Risk Research* 25 (8): 991–1007. https://doi.org/10.1080/13669877.2020.1864008.

Steele, J. 2004. *Risks and legal theory*. Oxford, UK: Hart Publishing.

Stephens, C. and C. Church. 2017. "Environmental justice and health." *International encyclopaedia of public health* 2nd ed., 499–506. https://doi.org/10.1016/B978-0-12-803678-5.00134-X.

Stirling, A. 2007. "Risk, precaution and science: Towards a more constructive policy debate." *EMBO reports* 8: 309–315.

Taubes, G. 2017. *The case against sugar*. New York: Knopf.

Van Asselt, M. and O. Renn. 2011. "Risk governance." *Journal of Risk Research* 1 (4). https://doi.org/10.1080/13669877.2011.553730.
Van Dijk, N., R. Gellert and K. Rommetveit. 2015. "A risk to a right? Beyond data protection risk assessments." *Computer Law & Security Review: The International Journal of Technology Law and Practice* 32 (2): 282–306. https://doi.org/10.1016/j.clsr.2015.12.017.
Von Schomberg, R. 2006. "The precautionary principle and its normative challenges." In *Implementing the precautionary principle—Perspectives and prospects*, ed. Fisher, E., J. Jones, J. and R. von Schomberg, 19–42. Cheltenham, UK: Edward Elgar.
WBGU - German Advisory Council on Global Change. 2000. World in Transition: Strategies for Managing Global Environmental Risks. Heidelberg and New York: Springer.
Weingart, P. 1999. "Scientific expertise and political accountability: Paradoxes of science in politics." *Science and Public Policy* 26 (3): 151–161.
Wildavsky, A. and K. Dake. 1990. "Theories of risk perception: Who fears what and why?" *Daedalus*, 119: 41–60.
Wolf, K.D. 2002. "Contextualizing normative standards for legitimate governance beyond the State." In *Participatory governance: Political and societal implications*, ed. Grote, J.R. and B. Gbikpi, 35–50. Opladen: Leske und Budrich.
World Health Organization—WHO. 1948. *Constitution of the world health organization*. http://www.who.int/governance/eb/who_constitution_en.pdf.
Wu, F., D. Jacobs, C. Mitchell, D. Miller and M. Karol. 2007. "Improving indoor environmental quality for public health: Impediments and policy recommendations." *Environmental health perspectives* 115 (6): 953.
Wynne, B. 1982. *Rationality and ritual: the Windscale inquiry and nuclear decision making in Britain*. British Society for the History of Science.
Wynne, B. 1992. "Uncertainty and environmental learning—Reconceiving science and policy in the preventive paradigm." *Global Environmental Change* 2 (2): 111–127.
Wynne, B. 1996. "May the sheep safely graze? A reflexive view of the expert-lay knowledge divide." In *Risk, environment and modernity*, ed. Lash, S., B. Szerszynski and B. Wynne, 44–83. Los Angeles: Sage.
Yassi, A., T. Kjellström, T. de Kok and T. Guidotti. 2001. "Nature of environmental health hazards." *Basic Environmental Health* 2 (1): 86. https://doi.org/10.1093/acprof:oso/9780195135589.003.0002.

CHAPTER 3

Identifying Dominant Models of Environmental Health Risk Governance

Abstract The 'problem' itself and its state-of-the-art are discussed in this chapter by investigating the arguably 'dominant' models of environmental risk governance and their criticisms. Particular attention is devoted to the discussion on the role of expert and lay knowledge in current risk governance. The central contribution that this chapter offers to the book is the argument that the current prevailing models of environmental risk governance often fail to include the input of the (lay) people concerned, who are often the most affected stakeholders. This acknowledgement triggers the suggestion that participatory practices of risk monitoring such as citizen sensing may—on one side—improve people's trust in risk policy and decision-making and—on the other side—effectively strengthen the ability of society to cope with complex risks.

Keywords Risk governance models · Expertise · Lay knowledge · Public participation

Dominant Models According to Millstone

In this chapter, what could be regarded as the prevailing models of (environmental health) risk governance will be inspected. The analysis is mainly based on the academic scholarship developed by Millstone in his work on grouping the dominant risk governance approaches under four 'models'.

A. Berti Suman, *Citizen Sensing for Risk Response*,
https://doi.org/10.1007/978-3-032-03939-2_3

Throughout this book, I mostly refer to 'risk governance frameworks' when I juxtapose citizen sensing to the institutional status-quo. Indeed, I wish to explore how citizen sensing can be inserted in and harmonized (if appropriate) with the current *rules* that govern risk governance. As here I discuss models instead, it is worth stressing the difference between *models* and *frameworks*. A 'model' is understood as a "[re]presentation in schematic form, often in a simplified way, of an existing or future [or, I add, desirable, when the model is normative] state or situation". A framework is instead "an entity [which] is, or contains, a (not completely detailed) structure or system for the realization of a defined result/goal".[1] The goal of a framework is indeed to provide a set of rules, procedures, and mechanisms guiding a certain process.[2] Thus, a model *represents* a state or situation, whereas a framework *circumscribes* it without necessarily representing anything. For example, a 'model' of a successful citizen sensing initiative for the aims of my research represents a basic or ideal type of citizen sensing initiatives having certain characteristics that allow them to contribute to environmental risk governance. Such a representation of the (or of an ideal) reality captured in the typology is clearly different from an integrative framework (yet inspires and serves it), that is a set of rules guiding the process of integration of citizen sensing into risk governance (developed in Berti Suman 2020).

In this and the following sections, the models will be criticized through the lens of the literature discussed above. The aim is to problematize for the dominant risk governance approaches and sketch a more inclusive framework where practices of citizen sensing may eventually play a role. In addition, these models will be investigated under the perspective of the contrast between *linear* and *non-linear* models of risk governance in order to understand the barriers that non-institutional practices of risk monitoring (may) face to find a place in such linear models.

Millston's categorization and illustration of four dominant models (Millstone 2010) is disentangled in order to answer three questions, on '*who* provides input to risk policy-making?'; 'who is in charge of implementing risk-related decisions?'; 'which element is missing in the governance of the risk?' The missing element identified in these models is

[1] See https://www.vanharen.net/blog/best-practice-model-framework-method-guidance-standard-towards-consistent-use-terminology/.

[2] See https://irgc.org/risk-governance/irgc-risk-governance-framework/.

that of the accountability of policy-makers and technocratic scientists to society in their decision-making. It will be shown that the models suffer from accountability deficit.

A premise must be made. I recognize that each model embeds an epistemological dilemma about how knowledge about reality enters policy (which has been extensively debated by Bijker et al. 2009). The two ends to this question are represented by science, on one side, or the people, on the other. Nevertheless, the distinction is not straightforward, but rather it is a matter of constant balance and power arrangements occurring between science and the public. The models are just crystallized representations of these dynamics, yet they can never be considered as capturing the reality of risk governance in its complexity. Bijker et al. (2009, 138) contributed to this reflection by disproving the assumption that there would be a gap between science, politics and the people.[3] Bonn et al. (2018, 468), in defending the potential of citizen science to foster innovation in science and policy, timely noted: "it is important to recognize, first, that *citizen science participants are often experts* in their respective fields, and sometimes have no parallel in academia" [emphasis added], which suggest that experts and sensing citizens are not two neatly distinct groups. These blurred boundaries are particularly crucial for understanding the frame of this research.

The goal of presenting Millstone's models is to understand which role, if any, citizen sensing *can play* in knowledge production for risk governance. In addition, it is questioned *for whom* the sensing citizens should be producing advice: for the scientists or directly for policy-makers? Furthermore, the question on *the legitimacy* of the source—science or lay knowledge—providing input to policy is addressed by exploring whether it is legitimate that science determines policy, or rather that people's input should shape it. I do not think such 'black or white' approaches are reasonable. Rather, a balance between different sources of knowledge should be sought. A possible question on the *right* model is not answered (although the second model is rejected) because it is not a matter of good, better, best, but rather of different perspectives. Thus, the contribution of my analysis is to understand how citizen sensing can help in enhancing current risk governance practices, starting from (the gaps of) the models outlined hereinafter.

[3] Their experience researching the functioning of the Health Council of the Netherlands showed that the advisory body constantly engage in relations with their publics.

Weber and Durkheim's Decisionist Model

According to the Millstone (2010, 2–3), a first model of risk governance would be the 'Weber and Durkheim's decisionist model'. The model is characterized by the aim of balancing the power of unaccountable bureaucrats (officials and *experts*)—here considered as the *institutional actors*—by subordinating their risk governance interventions to "*accountable*, democratically elected representatives" (Millstone 2010, 2–3). This model is based on having risk-related deliberations of bureaucrats always framed on "the goals and ends of policy *decisions* set by politically-accountable representatives" (thus *decisionistic*) (Millstone 2010, 2–3). Therefore, values and objectives shaping risk governance should rest in the hands of democratically elected leaders, while the bureaucrats would have the task to select the means to achieve such aims.

The Technocratic Model

The second model in Millstone's analysis (2010, 2–3), the 'technocratic model', reflects an opposite approach. Indeed, the model—developed in the nineteenth century by positivists Henri de Saint-Simon and Auguste Comte—strongly supports the supremacy of technical expertise in handling risks on behalf of society. In their opinion, experts (arguably, impartial) should replace elected representatives (accordingly, biased), because only this way accurate and scientifically informed decisions aimed at tackling risks can be adopted. An (exclusive) reliance on scientific and technical considerations on the risk at issue would guarantee a fair and appropriate risk-related decision-making process. According to Millstone's analysis (2010, 4), democratically elected representatives would have the sole task to recruit the best experts and follow their advice in designing risk policies.

The Inverted Decisionist Model

The third model in Millstone (2010, 6–7) has been defined as 'inverted decisionist' model or the 'Red Book model'. In this model, the input to policy-making is provided by science, supposedly free from policy advice, whereas policy-makers are in charge of implementing the decisions. Remarkably, the 'ends' (later framed as risk assessment) of the interventions are set by scientists, while policy determines the 'means' (later framed risk management). The regulatory interventions adopted as a result of this flow are informed by scientific facts and considerations provided by scientists, but also by social, political, ethical, economic and cultural considerations underlying policy decisions. This model originated in the U.S. in connection with the enactment of Freedom of Information Acts in the 1970s and with several judicial decisions related to access to information and risk governance/risk regulation, e.g., the Benzene case on the regulation of carcinogens (Postol and McElveen 1981). These events stressed the importance of a risk assessment based on facts and not on political considerations, and the need to differentiate risk *assessment* from its *management*. The reflections around this model stimulated the development of the so-called "Red Book" (also known as "Risk Assessment in the Federal Government: managing the process", U.S. National Research Council 1983). In the analysis of Gellert (2017, 45), the Red Book contributed to the debate on risk governance under two perspectives. First, it pinpointed how methodologically risk governance is based on a mix of toxicology (risk level) and epidemiology (risk effects). Secondly, it separated the risk assessment phase from the regulatory decision-making phase, leading to the outlined distinction between risk assessment and management.

The Co-dynamic Model

Lastly, Millstone presents the co-dynamic model (2010, 8–9), arguing: "scientific deliberations on risks in policy-making contexts never operate in a policy vacuum" (Millstone 2010, 8). Social assumptions and embedded values are always behind scientific and technical considerations. Consequently, experts and policy-makers alone cannot legitimate their choices, but they need to back their decisions on societal values. In the co-dynamic model, both science and policy are shaped by such values. In addition, a key characteristic of this model is the *reciprocal relationship* between science and policy-making: scientific choices must be supported by up-stream and down-stream policy decisions. The down-stream policies for risk governance of this model follow the Red Book model illustrated above, but complemented by 'high-level up-stream framing assumptions' based on societal values (Millstone 2010, 8).

Reading the Models Through Three Questions

The three questions outlined above are now applied to each model, through the support of graphical illustrations, i.e., Figs. 3.1, 3.2, 3.3, 3.4, and 3.5. Starting from the 'Weber and Durkheim's decisionist model', the three questions can be answered as follows:

- *Who provides input to risk policy-making?* The elected representatives, setting goals and ends of risk policies, basing their choices on societal values, experts' opinions, arguments of lobbies and constituents and on risk and harm information shaping the choice of values and objectives.
- *Who is in charge of implementing risk-related decisions?* Unaccountable bureaucrats (officials and experts).

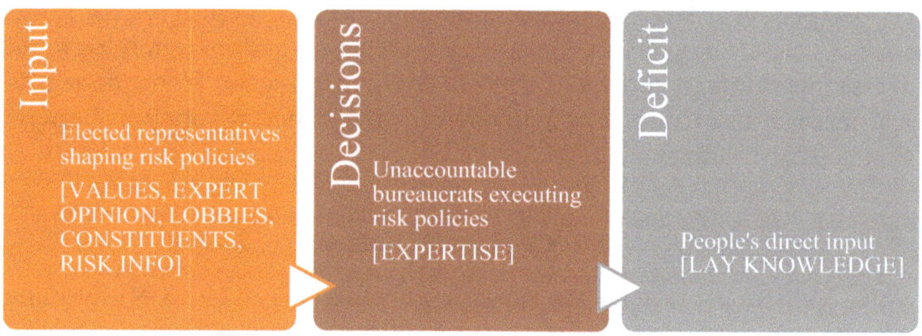

Fig. 3.1 A critical analysis of Weber and Durkheim's decisionist model

Fig. 3.2 A critical analysis of the technocratic model

Fig. 3.3 A critical analysis of the inverted decisionist model

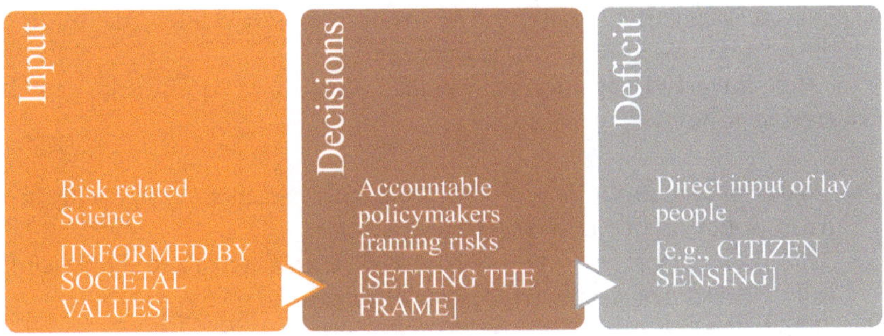

Fig. 3.4 A critical analysis of the co-dynamic model

- *Which element is missing in the governance of the risk?* The direct input of lay people, beyond the representative system of democracy (based on elected representatives).

This model suggests a risk governance system which is values-informed and accountable to the electorate, although not in the implementation of the decisions which is in the hand of unaccountable bureaucrats. A representative democracy, rather than more 'direct' forms of participation (entailed in citizen sensing practices), holds the primacy. Yet, also in this model one should not neglect the abilities of citizens to form lobbies, activists' groups and organize themselves in non-governmental organizations and influence the system by subjecting to scrutiny elected leaders.

The second model, the 'technocratic model', can instead be illustrated as follows:

- *Who provides input to risk policy-making?* The risk technocrats (recruited by elected representatives) which are experts presenting science as a fact.
- *Who is in charge of implementing risk-related decisions?* Bureaucrats, in charge of translating scientific input into risk policies.
- *Which element is missing in the governance of the risk?* The proactive role of elected representatives and any contribution from lay knowledge.

This model is essentially rejected in my frame as it denies the value of including lay knowledge in risk governance.

In the 'inverted decisionist model', the three questions can be answered as follows:

- *Who provides input to risk policy-making?* Science, supposedly free from policy advice (risk assessment).
- *Who is in charge of implementing risk-related decisions?* Democratically elected politicians (risk management).
- *Which element is missing in the governance of the risk?* The understanding that science cannot be neutral and values-free.

This model maintains both components, i.e., the scientific and the technical knowledge, and the role played by democratically elected leaders. However, it suggests that scientific and political deliberations take place in two *very different* compartments or, in other words, that science is not influenced by policy advice. Accordingly, while policy-making would be based on scientific risk assessment, science would not be influenced by political considerations and values, which is the main problem I identify in relation to this model.

The three dimensions of the fourth model, 'the co-dynamic model', can be listed as follows:

- *Who provides input to risk policy-making?* Science, framed by social assumptions and embedding societal values.

Fig. 3.5 Linear versus non-linear models of risk governance

- *Who is in charge of implementing risk-related decisions?* Accountable politicians, in charge of defining high-level up-stream risk framing assumptions (or 'risk assessment policy').
- *Which element is missing in the governance of the risk?* Also here, the direct contribution of lay people to the system (e.g., through citizen sensing).

The first and fourth models seem the ones reflecting to the greater extent the aims of this book. Yet, both models lack the direct input of lay people to risk governance, although in the fourth model this shortcoming is mitigated by mechanisms granting accountability of risk policy-makers.

The models more conflicting with the aims of my analysis are the second and third. The second model would represent what van Asselt and Vos (2008) defined as the 'technocratic handling' of risks. This *technocratic approach* corresponds to a linear way of dealing with risk governance on the basis of a standardized set of procedures for risk handling and on formalized responsibility for making risk-related decisions (van Asselt and Vos 2008). According to van Asselt and Vos (2008), the technocratic handling of the risk entails the reframing and *simplification* of complex risks with the aim of minimizing uncertainty. This, however, in the long-term enhances social conflicts over risk problems. Reducing complexity by presenting complex risks as simple could appear as a way to facilitate their governance. Nonetheless, the nuances generating complexity and uncertainty are *part of the problem* itself and proper governance cannot disregard them, as this would just worsen social frictions and divergences over the risk (van Asselt and Vos 2008). Rutz et al. (2013, 375) contributed to this discussion. On the basis of empirical research conducted on Dutch inspectorates with regards to youth poverty, the authors concluded that—for the sake of transmitting a sense of certainty—the institutional actors (in the case, the inspectorates) oversimplified the complexity behind the involvement of interested actors and disregarded their perspectives. In opposition to this approach, the authors argue that the inclusion of a variety of stakeholders is "essential in dealing with complexity, uncertainty and ambiguity", although their exclusion may make risk governance *simpler* and *faster* (Rutz et al. 2013, 377).

I endorse Millstone's critique to the third model (Millstone 2010, 7–8), which tackles specifically the separation between science and political considerations and values. This separation results in being problematic both conceptually and empirically. Conceptually, this division implies that the scientific experts would ultimately be those responsible for establishing the ends and goals of policy and policy-makers—elected and accountable to the people—would just have to select the means on the basis of scientific (values-informed) evidence. Nevertheless, intuitively and according to the general thinking, policy-makers are in charge of steering technology towards the values embedded in the society that they represent, whereas the experts are in charge of adapting technological and scientific processes to societal principles and norms. Most importantly, this model assumes that science can be a pure and objective representation of the reality, free from values. However, as discussed *infra*, no scientific statement can be "a purely intellectual process" (Wynne 1992, 281). Consequently, also the scientific input should be regarded as part of the "social package" (Wynne 1992, 282) containing not only scientific data but also values and power relationships. Thus, at a substantial level, scientific advice would not differ much from policy advice, as both are informed by end goals and are shaped by societal values. However, as their methods differ, their results and way of thinking will rest inherently different.

As illustrated above, the first model presents some elements that I endorse here, such as a risk governance system which is values-informed and accountable to the people. However, I reject the idea of the implementation of decisions in the hand of unaccountable bureaucrats. The fourth Millstone model is instead considered the most aligned with the goals of my analysis. Firstly, what is supported is the *reciprocal relationship* between science and policy-making. Secondly, I endorse the view that scientific choices must be supported by one up-stream and one down-stream risk governance approach, the first following the Red Book model illustrated above, but complemented by 'high-level up-stream framing assumptions' based on *societal values* (Millstone 2010, 8). Thirdly, it is crucial in the model the *mutual exchange of knowledge,* and the steering process between expert risk assessment and up-stream and down-stream risk management.

Millstone (2010, 9) analyses the four models not only theoretically, but also through examples, situating them in the context of food safety policy-making (with regards to food chemicals, which is a good example of a public health risk derived from environmental factors). The author mentions the intergovernmental organization Codex Alimentarius, formed in 1963 from the joint membership of the WHO and the United Nations Food and Agriculture Organization (FAO), with the mission to establish food safety standards for internationally traded commodities. The author illustrates how Codex decided to abandon the Red Book model to adopt the more flexible co-dynamic model. Furthermore, the organization *readapted* that model by substituting the 'up-stream framing assumptions' with the expression 'risk assessment policy'. The consequence of this innovation was the introduction of new principles orienting risk governance, which read as follows:

> "(1) Determination of risk assessment policy should be included as a specific component of risk management. (2) Risk assessment policy should be established by risk managers in advance of risk assessment, in consultation with risk assessors and all other interested parties. This procedure aims at ensuring that the risk assessment is systematic, complete, unbiased and transparent. (3) The mandate given by risk managers to risk assessors should be as clear as possible. (4) Where necessary, risk managers should ask risk assessors to evaluate the potential changes in risk resulting from different risk management options" [emphasis added] (Codex Alimentarius Commission 2003, Appendix IV par. 13-16).

The attention paid to the inclusion of 'all other interested parties' seems a step towards an integrative and flexible model of risk governance.

The four models illustrated through Millstone have been shaped by very heterogeneous historical, social and political factors. The description here provided thus just a simplified and schematic presentation of possible (present, past but also future) ways to approach and structure risk governance. As the notion of governance and of risk governance, these models not only have a descriptive but also a normative scope. Interpreting Millstone's critique to the models and the use of the word 'should', I posit that these models also have a prescriptive goal since they show contrasting views on how science, policy and the publics should address risk governance. Both in their descriptive and normative understanding, these models manifest in the reality as exemplifications thereof but also as judgmental approaches to the problem of risk governance. In terms of their manifestations in reality, some models are more confined in time and space, other alternated over the course of history, while yet other models coexisted over the same period, but in different sectors or (geographical) contexts. In some instances, the reality of risk governance was the manifestation of a mix of models. This is likely because—as stressed above—the one-size-fits-all approach cannot handle the complexity of risk governance. Instead, complex, uncertain and ambiguous risks ask for flexible and adaptive models, which can take inspiration from the 'classical' models, but also have to be *reinvented* in consideration of the circumstances. Also considering this need for adaptation, I view the co-dynamic model as the preferable approach.

In addition to the endorsement of an 'adaptive co-dynamic model', I consider nodal the contrast between *linear* models of risk governance (as, for example, the technocratic model or the inverted decisionist) and *non-linear* models reflecting unplanned and non-institutionalized human interventions into the system (Renn et al. 2011, 239). The 'linear' way(s) of governing environmental risks to public health has often corresponded to the approach predominantly adopted by the competent institutional actors. Such an institutional approach to, for instance, monitoring an environmental risk can be schematized as based on high quality monitoring equipment, controlled by a single governmental body, requiring considerable expenses and continuous labour, which often leads to low spatial and temporal resolution (Mead et al. 2013; Berti Suman 2018a). The non-linear models based on a multi-actor and multilateral approach (including the citizens) could instead include citizen sensing practices, as I will explain further on.

As van Asselt and Renn put it (2011, 442),

> "Risk governance is not a linear, sequential three-stage process of risk assessment, management, and communication, but it is dynamic and requires *interlinked and iterative processes*. Although it may still be useful

> to distinguish assessment (examining the risks and benefits) from management (identifying regulatory options), it is important to realize that they can and should not be viewed as unconnected activities to be carried out in different realms" [emphasis added].

The authors' opinion corroborates one of my main arguments, i.e., that classical models of risk governance should be challenged and reshaped to *include* non-linear and non-institutionalized practices that, nevertheless, have the considerable potential to enhance the governance of complex, uncertain and ambiguous risks.

In the figure, the linear model is represented by a decisional hub, posed in a top position (the dot), that exercises its decision-making power (the arrow) over a multitude of grassroots' actors (the horizontal line). In the second figure, the various dots represented multiple decisional fulcra, some placed in top positions, some in intermediate and bottom positions, sharing decisional power, which is represented by the looping arrows. Fisher (2017, 125) (also in Berti Suman 2018a) recently discussed the dichotomy between top-down risk regulation, conceived as a linear pattern and more participatory approaches, exemplified as "looping arrows going all over the place representing risk regulation as an iterative process that constantly involved many scientific, socio-political and other inputs" (e.g., input from civil society). Fisher's reflections too seem to support the argument that the engagement of non-institutional actors in risk governance can *improve* societal risk coping strategies (Berti Suman 2018a).

The Gaps and Shortcomings of the Described Models

In this section, several alleged weaknesses of the models will be analysed, devoting particular attention to the aptness of such models to cope with complex and systemic risks. The need to 'update' the models in view of a more flexible and inclusive approach to risk governance will be stressed (Renn et al. 2011, 232). This analysis supports the argument on the potential of citizen sensing in complementing the traditional models of environmental health risk governance, thus enhancing its legitimacy and accountability. Under this perspective, I build on relevant socio-legal scholarship on the topic, represented by authors like Renn, Klinke, van

Asselt, Wolf, Bulkeley, Brooks, Adger, Kramarz, Beierle, Cayford, Park and Gellert.

Demands for greater accountability in the governance of shared risks have been said to continuously increase (Kramarz and Park 2016, 5). Risk governance has been framed as a way to make risk handling more *legitimate and acceptable* by the public (Gellert 2017, 51). Nonetheless, the classic models of risk governance—based on risk assessment, management and communication—have often been criticized as obsolete. Renn et al. (2011, 231–232) argue that such models, resulting from an evolution dating back to decades ago, are outdated and insufficient to cope with the challenges posed by the risks of contemporary society. The classic models seem too narrow, when confronted with the proliferation of non-institutional stakeholders willing and having the capacity to monitor and communicate risks (also in Berti Suman, 2018b). The dominance of state agencies would miss the emergence of informal actors that, regardless the institutional acceptance thereof or desirability, want to play a role on the risk arena.

The 'reliance on expanded inclusion of stakeholders' in risk governance (Renn et al. 2011, 232) is conceived here not only as a fact that governors have to cope with, but also as an opportunity for strengthening the current approaches to risk governance. It is indeed empirically proven that multi-stakeholder governance of risks has the potential to reduce the conflict surrounding a risky situation and to improve the perception of *legitimacy* of the final decision (Beierle and Cayford 2002; Berti Suman 2018b).

At the political level, similar discussions are ongoing. The WHO in its publication "Health and environment: communicating the risks" (2013, 1) underlines how nowadays "public administrations at all levels must often manage ***complex*** situations related to environmental determinants of health, often ***surrounded by controversy***" [emphasis added]. The controversy in these situations would rapidly escalate due to "increased sensitivity in the face of uncertain risks, uneven distribution of risks and benefits, and ***decreasing trust*** in authorities and entities involved in making decisions influencing public health" [emphasis added] (WHO 2013, 1). The trust element among stakeholders affected by or dealing with risks once again results in being crucial. In such controversial scenarios surrounding complex risks, the separation between scientific and technical knowledge and society is not advisable. Lay people are increasingly becoming engaged in scientific research and, consequently, also risk governance should give them a role. As laypersons are increasingly becoming able to report risk information and track risks (as already demonstrated years ago by Boulos et al. (2011), right at the advent of the smartphone 'hype'), the monopoly of expert knowledge is falling apart. Moreover, the growing scientific uncertainty of today's risks shows that risk governance cannot only be based on 'sound science', arguably free from values.

In cases of the limitedness or even absence of scientific knowledge over a risk (e.g., data on the potential impacts of the environmental factor *x* on the health of the population *y*), it is difficult to assess the possible consequences of an event and therefore to define the proper governance strategy. In these instances, the dominant trend in the classic models of risk governance would be the described *reduction of complexity* approach where the causal chain between a hazardous agent and its impact on a risk-absorbing target is translated into a simplistic unidirectional causal relationship (Renn et al. 2011, 234; Berti Suman 2018b). Although the very notion of risk governance arose from the necessity to cope with complex risks, the dominant approaches handle risks as if they were *simple* (Renn et al. 2011, 236). However, this over-simplification brings about incomplete or inadequate governance strategies. As stressed above, treating complex risks as simple do not reduce the complexity but just postpones the issue to a later stage, often in the strategy implementation phase (Renn et al. 2011, 236; Berti Suman 2018b). As Renn et al. (2011, 236) underline, this reduction of risk complexity often produces "social amplification or irresponsible attenuation of the risk, sustained controversy, deadlocks, legitimacy problems, unintelligible decision-making, trade conflicts, border conflicts, expensive rebound measures, and lock-ins".

For example, taking the case of air pollution (as illustrated in Berti Suman 2018b), if the institutional measurements show that the operations of the company *x* do not affect the community *y*, but the community still reports ailments, in a simplistic model there would be no room for addressing the perceived air pollution problem. Nevertheless, this perceived harm will give rise to a social conflict, when the people feel that their claims are disregarded in the institutional risk governance strategy. The institutions, sooner or later, will be forced to listen to the people and eventually a strategy to cope with the (real or perceived) risk will have to be designed. Consequently, it seems reasonable to wonder why not to adopt this inclusive approach from the beginning. However, it could be also argued that such an approach may lead to a disproportionate number of claims from citizens, in the absence of mechanisms to prevent frivolous claims. I also tackle the issue of how to ensure that citizen inclusion in risk governance is not abused by the citizens themselves, stressing the importance of scientific strength in reporting risks through citizen sensing.

The present research indeed makes a case for the adoption of citizen sensing to fill gaps deriving, for example, from uncertainty in scientific knowledge, not citizen sensing for creating unfounded claims (or, using popular terms, 'fake news' or 'conspiracy theories'). Yet, I acknowledge that often what is a true claim and what is a fabricated one may be a matter of perspective, and an objective judgement may be undermined by political beliefs and partisan attitudes. In a post-truth age, where the foundations of scientific authority are eroded and official science is often attacked,[4] citizen science may be vulnerable to manipulations that want to make appear as scientific what is just fake news. I suggest that gatekeeping organizations that can ensure an independent oversight such as Citizen Science Associations worldwide may step in and 'regulate' from below the field.

On a different note, I wish to stress the potential of citizen sensing beyond producing data as, in recent times, governance and regulatory struggles on environmental health risks have been caused by uncertainty, rather than by scarcity of data over risks. Situations of uncertainty are rarely solved by more data. Consequently, citizen sensing is here presented not as a tool to increase the availability of already abundant data, but as a means to *foster a dialogue* aimed at disentangling uncertainties. Nevertheless, in some cases more data, in particular those produced by non-institutional sources such as the citizens, can still help to address risk challenges. For example, in the Safecast case, targeting post-Fukushima radiation monitoring, the scarcity of reliable data available to the public on radiation-safe areas created uncertainties to which some citizens responded by creating an alternative radiation monitoring network.

On the side of the review of relevant literature on the topic, discussions with experts in the field enriched my understanding of the debate.

[4] For a focus on citizen science and Post-Normal Science, see https://povesham.wordpress.com/2020/09/26/citizen-science-post-normal-science-zones/ and Haklay et al. (2023).

Among my communications with experts, I have discussed[5] the issues of accountability gaps in the dominant risk governance structures with historian Ulf Schmidt.[6] Although Schmidt focuses on a different research perspective, namely, the history of medicine during the Third Reich (including human experimentation, the Nuremberg Doctors' Trial and the Nuremberg Code), he resonated with me on the issues of 'closed-doors' processes *banning public oversight* and thus accountability scrutiny in complex (medical and) public health decision-making processes. In his book "Justice at Nuremberg", Schmidt (2004) investigates how the Nuremberg Code, for the first time, subjected medicine and physicians to an *accountability scrutiny*. The Code stimulated a debate on human rights and ethics in medical science. A shock, such as the acknowledgement of the Nazi medical atrocities, urged a ground-breaking change in how medical practice and research was conducted. Similar shocks—though less outrageous—occurred in the history of environmental health policies. Scepticism and distrust from the public opinion towards institutions peaked after scandals in the sector and the release of documents triggering public outrage, such as the WHO global report on trends in tobacco smoking 2000–2025,[7] the outbreak of the avian influenza and the relative guidelines issued by the WHO,[8] and more recently the 'Glyphosate Saga' and the 'Monsanto Papers'.[9] Such events showed weaknesses of the institutional oversight and stimulated decision-makers to consider public participation as a means to regain trust from the public but also as a form of control over formerly 'closed-doors' governance processes.

In view of what I argued, it is pertinent to conclude that *structural and procedural* changes in traditional risk governance are needed (and, in part, ongoing). Van Asselt and Renn (2011, 443) stressed such a

[5] The discussion occurred on August 7, 2018, during my research visit at the Brocher Foundation (Geneva, Switzerland), a research centre focused on the ethical, legal and social implications of recent medical research and new technologies.

[6] Professor of Modern History and Director of the Centre for the History of Medicine, Ethics and Medical Humanities at the University of Kent.

[7] See http://www.who.int/tobacco/publications/surveillance/reportontrendstobacco smoking/en/.

[8] See http://www.who.int/influenza/resources/documents/guidelinestopics/en/.

[9] See https://corporateeurope.org/food-and-agriculture/2018/03/what-monsanto-papers-tell-us-about-corporate-science; and https://corporateeurope.org/food-and-agricu lture/2015/04/glyphosate-saga-independent-scientific-advice-according-germany-uk.

need by developing "alternative concepts and approaches to [face] uncertain, complex, and/or ambiguous risks". The advised structural changes would reflect "the ability to design and *incorporate the necessary steps* [to] allow risk managers to reduce, mitigate or control the occurrence of harmful outcomes resulting from *collectively relevant* risk problems in a[...] *fair* manner" [emphasis added] (Brooks and Adger 2005, 165–181; Renn et al. 2011, 236). The incorporation of the 'necessary steps' could arguably coincide with the inclusion of grassroots-generated knowledge through citizen sensing practices. In addition, particularly timely appears the reflection of Jasanoff (2005, 267) who points out that the expert has a double responsibility: first, "to be knowledgeable" and, second, to be "accountable".

Although it is impossible to define *the best* model of risk governance—risk governance would not even be a model, but rather a 'paradigm' that should orient risk governors (van Asselt and Renn 2011, 439)—a reflection on possible guiding principles to achieve a more inclusive risk governance is advisable. These principles, developed by risk governance scholars (van Asselt and Renn 2011, 439–443), can be summarized as follows:

- *Mutual communication* emerges as a decisive factor for successful risk governance, because of its interlink with the establishment of trust. In addition, as van Asselt and Renn (2011) note, communication implies social learning and therefore—I add—also the inclusion of social actors in the learning process over risks, regardless their level of education. The importance of risk communication will be further addressed *infra* in this book, for the importance it plays in terms of mitigating or worsening conflicts over risks. An illustration of this is the case of shale gas extraction which, in the past, was frequently conducted without (proper or any) communication to potentially interested civil society actors as it simply was not considered a problematic environmental domain. Only when civil society started raising claims, issues about miscommunication over the side effects of fracking emerged (Stasik 2017).
- *Integration* also appears fundamental, representing the need to collect and synthesize all relevant knowledge and experience from various sources, including articulations of risk perceptions and values. The principle reflects the need for risk governance that goes beyond the sole reliance on scientific knowledge, to include

other important elements—for example, tolerability and equity—that are determinant in the governance of complex risks. These 'complementary' elements often derive from 'experiential' and 'tacit (indigenous)' knowledge (van Asselt and Renn 2011, 442). The principle calls for an 'holistic approach' to framing, appraising, characterizing, evaluating and managing risks (Zinn and Taylor-Gooby 2006). Such an approach would indeed reject the separation between risk assessment and risk management and push for an integrated risk governance process.

- *Reflection* which stands for the importance not to 'routinize' risk governance. Especially in case of uncertain, complex and ambiguous risks, standard patterns of risk governance do not hold. Rather, a collective reflection with a broader number of affected stakeholders is needed to balance pros and cons of a certain decision over a risk. This approach has been defined as 'precaution-based risk governance' (Van Dijk et al. 2011, 451–466).

The presented principles will facilitate and inspire my following analysis. Nevertheless, the importance of flexibility in risk governance strategies will require, over the research process, the adaptation and constant rediscussion of these key principles.

Case Insight 2: Scepticism Towards Traditional Approaches in Governing Risks

Empirical analysis performed in the exploratory data collection phase of this book showed a high discontent towards the institutional way of responding to the risk at issue. Also, the targeted survey deployed in a second stage of this research with a wider pool of citizen sensing initiatives' participants showed a similar trend.[The italics in the text are added and indicate particularly relevant wording].

Lamenting a Reactive Rather Than Proactive Approach

Participants from the I-REACT initiative,[10] the first European-wide platform to integrate emergency management-data coming from (also) citizen sensing, showed scepticism by arguing that "governments work on a *knee-jerk response, spending more money on recovery than they do on*

[10] See http://project.i-react.eu/.

prevention" and also that "[we] need more regulations and things that force citizens to change." Overall, participants consulted were upset as governments "do not listen to constituents who they represent". The problem was identified in the fact that "there is a lack of understanding of how policies can be informed by solid scientific information." The reason why "governments do not inform their policy decisions on solid scientific information" is because they "*do not trust* science", according to a volunteer. These quotes show a worrisome trend of citizens that feel that their institutions not only fail to properly represent their desires but are not even well informed in deploying their actions, as they 'disregard' science altogether.

The majority of Safecast volunteers showed to be dissatisfied too with the government's conduct, yet they acknowledged that part of the problem when risk governance fails is also the low awareness of the people. "Lack of focus on data gathering and transparency by governments" is a problem, a volunteer noted, but also "*lack of awareness of citizens* on the risks of exposure to bad air and radiation." Other quotes from Safecast volunteers also convey this sense of scepticism, such as "If I thought there were people [in the competent institutions] doing it [i.e., properly monitoring risk] *then I wouldn't be doing it myself*"; "Trust is earned, by and large the government hasn't earned it"; and "We [i.e., Safecast] are doing it better than they are."

Intentionally Hiding Data

A sense of 'conspiracy' of the government against its citizens and the environment appears in the words of a participant from PurpleAir,[11] a citizen-based air quality sensor network providing real-time measurement of air quality on a public map. The respondent noted: "The government of the United States of America is dominated by the white supremacists [...] whose network fund political campaigns through so-called dark money. [The white supremacist] *has dominated the Environmental Protection Agency* [...] killing off Federal government response capability [in order] to enable him to pollute at will." Safecast participants too refer to a risk of intentional data cover-up by the responsible institutions. They pinpointed the problem of "lack of transparency and use of open data protocols [which] *make it hard to get access to environmental data or*

[11] See https://www2.purpleair.com/.

verify how the data was collected. Moreover [...]data [over] risk[s] may *be unavailable when it matters or be removed from public access due to changes in political views*". Overall, "there are too many conflicts of interest to make" good risk governance happen, "Fukushima Daiichi is a living example of that process not working".

In addition to these concerns, the law seems unhelpful, as reflected by a respondent from Safecast who argued: "In Japan, secrecy laws may interfere with our operations (as these are opaque, [it is] not possible to assess their actual risk [for our operations])" and referred to a "long history of closed approaches [...] *assuming the public doesn't need to know or isn't able to understand.*" Compared to an obscure risk governance, Safecast is meant to "spread non opinionated radiation data through devices developed by [the volunteers] themselves. *Japanese government could not manage to do this but citizen scientists* [...] *have achieved this for free which is amazing.*" Scepticism towards institutions is accompanied by a sense of proudness towards the civic response through citizen sensing.

References

Beierle, T.C., and J. Cayford. 2002. *Democracy in practice: Public participation in environmental Decisions*. Washington, DC: Resources for the Future.

Berti Suman, A. 2020. *Sensing the risk. A case for integrating citizen sensing into risk governance*. Tilburg, Open Press TiU. ISBN: 978-94-6240-631-5.

Berti Suman, A. 2018a. "Challenging risk governance patterns through citizen sensing: The Schiphol Airport case." *International Review of Law, Computers & Technology* 32 (1). https://doi.org/10.1080/13600869.2018.1429186.

Berti Suman, A. 2018b. "The smart transition: an opportunity for a sensor-based public-health risk governance?" *International Review of Law, Computers & Technology* 32 (2–3), *Special issue on 'Smart Cities or Smart Machines: Data Infrastructures and the Rule(s) of Law'*: 257–274. https://doi.org/10.1080/13600869.2018.1463961.

Bijker, W.E., R. Bal, and R. Hendriks. 2009. *The paradox of scientific authority: The role of scientific advice in democracies*. Cambridge, MA: The MIT Press.

Bonn, A., et al. 2018. "Citizen science to foster innovation in open science, society and policy: Innovation in Open Science, Society and Policy". In *Citizen science: Innovation in Open Science, Society and Policy*, ed. S. Hecker et al. London: UCL Press. https://doi.org/10.14324/111.9781787352339.

Boulos, K., et al. 2011. "Crowdsourcing, citizen sensing and sensor web technologies for public and environmental health surveillance and crisis management: Trends, OGC standards and application examples." *International Journal of Health Geographics* 67 (10). https://doi.org/10.1186/1476-072X-10-67.

Brooks, M., and W.N. Adger. 2005. "Assessing and enhancing adaptive capacity." In *Adaptation policy frameworks for climate change: Developing strategies, policies and measures*, ed. K. Chopra et al., 165–181. Cambridge: Cambridge University Press.

Codex Alimentarius Commission. 2003. *Procedural Manual* 13th ed. http://www.codexalimentarius.net/web/procedural_manual.jsp.

Fisher, E. 2017. "Framing risk regulation: A critical reflection." *European Journal of Risk Regulation* 4 (2): 125–132. https://doi.org/10.1017/S1867299X00003299.

Gellert, R. 2017. Understanding the risk-based approach to data protection: An analysis of the links between law, regulation, and risk. Thesis submitted in view of obtaining the degree of Doctor of Philosophy in Law, Vrije Universiteit Brussel. *Later published as: Gellert, R. 2020.* The risk-based approach to data protection. Oxford: Oxford University Press.

Haklay, M., A. König, F. Moustard, and N. Aspee. 2023. "Citizen science and Post-Normal Science's extended peer community: Identifying overlaps by mapping typologies." *Futures* 150. https://doi.org/10.1016/j.futures.2023.103178.

Jasanoff, S. 2005. *Designs on nature: Science and democracy in Europe and the United States*. Princeton University Press.

Kramarz, T. and S. Park. 2016. "Accountability in Global Environmental Governance: A Meaningful Tool for Action?". *Global Environmental Politics* 16(2).https://doi.org/10.1162/GLEP_a_00349.

Mead, M.I., et al. 2013. "The use of electrochemical sensors for monitoring urban air quality in lowcost, high-density networks." *Atmospheric Environment* 70: 186–203. https://doi.org/10.1016/j.atmosenv.2012.11.060.

Millstone, E. 2010. *The evolution of risk assessment paradigms: in theory and in practice*. SPRU—Science and Technology Policy Research, University of Sussex.

Postol, L.P., and J.C. McElveen. 1981. "The Supreme Court's decision in the benzene case." *Occupational Health Safety* 50 (5): 37–40.

Renn, O., A. Klinke, and M. van Asselt. 2011. "Coping with complexity, uncertainty and ambiguity in risk governance: A synthesis." *Ambio* 40: 231–246. https://doi.org/10.1007/s13280-010-0134-0.

Rutz, S.I., S.A. Adams, S.E. Buitendijk, P.B.M. Robben and A.A. de Bont. 2013. "Hiding complexity, uncertainty and ambiguity: how inspectorates simplify issues to create enforceable action". *Health, Risk & Society* 15(4): 363-379.https://doi.org/10.1080/13698575.2013.796343.

Schmidt, U. 2004. *Justice at Nuremberg: Leo Alexander and the Nazi Doctors' Trial*. London: Palgrave Macmillan.

Stasik, A. 2017. "Global controversies in local settings: Anti-fracking activism in the Era of Web 2.0." *Journal of Risk Research*: 1–17. https://doi.org/10.1080/13669877.2017.1313759.

US National Research Council. 1983. *Risk Assessment in the Federal Government: Managing the process*. Washington, DC: The National Academies Press.

Van Asselt, M., and E. Vos. 2008. "Wrestling with uncertain risks: EU regulation of GMOs and the uncertainty paradox." *Journal of Risk Research* 11 (1): 281–300.

Van Asselt, M., and O. Renn. 2011. "Risk governance." *Journal of Risk Research* 14 (4): 431–449. https://doi.org/10.1080/13669877.2011.553730.

Van Dijk, H.F.G., et al. 2011. "The role of scientific advisory bodies in precaution-based risk governance illustrated with the issue of uncertain health effects of electromagnetic fields." *Journal of Risk Research* 14 (4): 451–466. https://doi.org/10.1080/13669877.2011.553729.

World Health Organization—WHO. 2013. *Health and environment: Communicating the risks*. Italy: Grafiche Antiga Spa.

Wynne, B. 1992. "Misunderstood misunderstanding: Social identities and public uptake of science." *Public Understanding of Science* 1 (3): 281–304. https://doi.org/10.1088/0963-6625/1/3/004.

Zinn, J.O., and P. Taylor-Gooby. 2006. "Risk as an interdisciplinary research area." In *Risk in social science*, ed. P. Taylor-Gooby and J. O. Zinn, 20–53. Oxford: Oxford University Press.

CHAPTER 4

Hypothesizing a New Approach to Risk Governance Based on Citizen Sensing

Abstract In this chapter, the fundamental debate currently ongoing on the role of expert and lay knowledge in risk governance is explored. A 'theory of change' is outlined by hypothesizing a new approach to risk governance based on citizen sensing, and inspecting its theoretical grounding and the need for empirical analysis. Here, the literature review is complemented by three in-depth, semi-structured, face-to-face expert interviews. The experts came from the policy sector and from academia, respectively an expert of Risk Governance and an expert of Citizen Science from the Dutch National Institute for Public Health and the Environment (RIVM), and an expert of Responsible Innovation and of Urban Innovation theories from Delft University of Technology. These experts are interviewed to get insights from the institutional arena and from the academic sector on the potential of citizen sensing for environmental risk governance, within the framework of innovation in governance of environmental and public health issues.

Keywords Theory of change · Policy uptake · Governance innovation · Expert interviews

A. Berti Suman, *Citizen Sensing for Risk Response*,
https://doi.org/10.1007/978-3-032-03939-2_4

The Role of Expert and Lay Knowledge in Current Risk Governance

This section discusses the role reserved to expert and lay knowledge in today's risk governance as a needed preliminary to stage to approach a proposed 'theory of change'. It partially draws on Bijker et al. (2009) reflections developed in the book "The Paradox of Scientific Authority. The Role of Scientific Advice in Democracies". The authors have studied the functioning of the Health Council of the Netherlands (the *Gezondheidsraad*), an independent advisory body providing solicited and unsolicited advice to the Dutch ministers and Parliament on matters of public health. The Council represented a strategic research site to investigate the role of scientific advice in modern policy-making. The authors questioned the authority of the Council (specifically, the *policy uptake* of its advisory reports) and extended their reflections to the general scientific authority in modern technological cultures. In line with my research focus, one of the areas in which the Council works is situated at the intersection of health and the environment (e.g., health-related risks of zinc, pesticides and electromagnetic fields). An additional contact point with my research is the focus of the authors on those instances in which scientific advice is given on risks surrounded by cognitive and/or normative *uncertainty* and that heavily impact collective interests and values (e.g., the effects of chemicals on human health). The paradox disentangled by Bijker et al. (2009) is that the more uncertain a problem is, the more demanded is the scientific input, yet also the more questioned the authority of such scientific input will be. The authors state: "as soon as advice is given, *citizens,* politicians, and non-governmental organizations comment on, *criticize,* or lend *additional support* to the scientists' report" [emphasis added] (Bijker et al. 2009, 1). According to the authors, this happens because science in such situations is 'instrumentalized' as a catalyst for controversies. In other words, science becomes a fulcrum of controversies because *called upon* in political matters (Weingart 1999).

Spruijt et al. (2014, 1) brought forward these reflections debating the controversial roles of scientists as "policy advisers on complex issues". The authors performed a literature review (of post-normal science, STS, science-policy studies, politics of expertise and risk governance literature) focusing specifically on the factors influencing the role of science in policy-making. From the analysis of the literature, they concluded that the role of experts is influenced by the context, the type of problem (simple or complex) and by other parties (*the public* and other stakeholders). Moreover, other factors, such as personal values, would strongly influence the role of science in policy-making. As noted by Bijker et al. (2009, 65) "scientific knowledge is not automatically policy-relevant knowledge", thus the importance of the 'human factor' entailed in translating scientific inputs in relevant information for policies. Spruijt et al. (2014) claimed the scarcity of empirical underpinning of the factors shaping the political role of science and of the differences in experts' roles. My research aims to contribute to this knowledge gap.

I stressed above that Bijker et al. (2009) devote particular attention to uncertain and ambiguous risk problems, where they envisage *a need* for participatory approaches. I situate citizen sensing as a phenomenon potentially at the centre of the debate over risk-associated cognitive and normative uncertainty. I posit that citizen sensing (eventually, yet not always) could meet this need for participatory approaches and mitigate conflicts associated with uncertainties. According to Rutz et al. (2013, 365), risk, referring to the "extent and nature of the problem", relates to the *ontological* sphere. Cognitive uncertainty, instead, would be "the lack of comprehensive knowledge" on the extent and nature of the risk. Cognitive uncertainty is often accompanied by normative uncertainty framed as the "values, assumptions and judgements about the risk problem and the desired prospects" (Rutz et al. 2013, 365). Both cognitive and normative uncertainty fall within the *epistemological* sphere and are said to often "cut across the traditional jurisdictions of organizations and cross the traditional boundaries between sectors" (Rutz et al. 2013, 365). These uncertainties thus push for a reconsideration of traditional organizational and institutional structures. Citizen sensing could be read as one of the manifestations of such institutional *transformation* of how society is facing cognitive and normative uncertainty As Rutz et al. stressed (2013, 366), "an essential aspect of dealing with complexity, uncertainty and ambiguity is the *inclusion* of *experiences and knowledge* of experts, stakeholders and the *general public*" [emphasis added].

The discussion on the boundaries and connections between expert science and lay knowledge in my research is also inspired by theories on boundary work (Gieryn 1983, 1999) and boundary objects (Star and Griesemer 1989). Particularly timely to this research is the study on how boundaries—in this case, between *expert and lay knowledge*—are established and how these separated worlds are connected through 'coordination mechanisms' identified in 'boundary objects' (Star and

Griesemer 1989). Another example of boundary work regards the divide and subsequent coordination between science and policy processes (Bijker et al. 2009, 45) or the division between science and 'non-science' (defined by Bijker et al. 2009, 144, as knowledge practices not characterized by the reliance on a scientific method, that cannot be falsified and that do not produce heuristic paradigms). In Chapter 5 of their book, Bijker et al. (2009) illustrate effectively these boundaries and boundary work through the analysis of how the Council, which in principle should not care about how its advice is being taken up by the government, cares to ensure a meaningful 'landing' of the advice. That the boundaries are evident is the fact that once the Council gives its advice to the government its official role is finished (the boundaries). Yet, de facto, the Council later on engages in policy-making effectiveness by repairing misinterpretations and advocating for the intended message (Bijker et al. 2009, 18), thus performing this work of 'coordination'.

Furthermore, in order to identify features of the world 'within the boundaries' (e.g., science), it is worthwhile to investigate the ways in which the boundaries between science and lay knowledge are "drawn, strategically deployed, and monitored" (Bijker et al. 2009, 144). This work of *setting boundaries* between science and surrounding worlds has been regarded as aimed at strengthening and reaffirming the authority of science (Shackley and Wynne 1996, 280; Bijker et al. 2009, 148). However, this effort of drawing boundaries can also be considered part of a work of *coordination*, aimed at negotiating "uncertainty that spans the boundary between science and policy" (Shackley and Wynne 1996, 280). Such a work would indeed have a twofold aim: first, boundaries are drawn to separate two worlds; then, reaffirming the distinctions between the two separated worlds, links to coordinate them are established (Bijker et al. 2009, 149). Law (2015, 15) also engages in discussing boundaries and connection mechanisms in a passage where he defines 'knowledge spaces' as:

> "Particular arrays of subjects, objects, expressions or representations, imaginaries, and institutions [which] set more or less permeable *boundaries* to the possible and the accessible; they are defined by *patterns of relations* which enact those gradients of possibility and accessibility; and they *intersect with* and are implicated in the generation of *alternative knowledge spaces* [...]". [emphasis added]

The sensing citizens in my frame, juxtaposing it to Law's argument, would be these arrays of subjects with their own expressions that explore and intersect boundaries with policy and expert science to propose their alternative knowledge spaces.

Especially relevant to the discussion of lay knowledge at the intersection of science and policy is also the work of Wynne (1992) with regards to the public uptake of science. The author takes the case of the Cumbrian sheep farmers' reception of scientific advice regarding restrictions on sheep sales as consequence of the Chernobyl radioactive fallout (Wynne 1992, 1996). Wynne describes the ban imposed on the sales of Cumbrian sheep for the levels of radio-caesium found in the soil where the sheep were grazing, allegedly consequent to the 1986 Chernobyl cloud which moved to Northern and Western Europe. Because of the (indefinite) ban, the farmers suffered serious economic losses as they could only sell their sheep's wool at extremely low price, because the wool was marked by the 'experts' as contaminated. The *specialist lay knowledge* of the farmers was completely neglected by the scientists as considered unfounded and ignorant. The experts did not feel any need to "integrate it with the science in order to manage the emergency properly" (Wynne 1992, 295). The farmers thus suffered twice, not only for the economic losses, but also for being excluded from the debate on how to deal with the problem of the contamination. Ultimately, it turned out that the experts were wrong on two aspects. First, the methods used to test the soil where the sheep grazed were inappropriate for Cumbrian soil. Secondly, the real cause of the contamination was *not* the Chernobyl fallout, but instead the United Kingdom (UK) Sellafield nuclear reprocessing complex. Wynne (1992) illustrates how many farmers actually were right as they believed the contamination was from Sellafield and not from Chernobyl at all. The Chernobyl accident was in fact the excuse to 'cover' a long-lasting controversy surrounding the effects of the first nuclear complex.

From the case study, Wynne shows the clash between 'external' to the context (and arguably *imposed*) scientific knowledge and local knowledge (Wynne 1992, 281). The credibility and trustworthiness of the scientific advice seems at stake. A science *blind* to the needs but also precious knowledge of the people fails in properly facing and communicating risks. It is argued that "risk communication or any scientific communication is never and can never be a purely intellectual process" (Wynne 1992, 281). In conveying scientific knowledge over risks, experts should take into account a whole "social package" (Wynne 1992, 282) containing not only the data on reality and the scientific data, but also values, social relationships, impressions and experiences. As wisely underlined by Wynne (1992, 283), a "traditional lay culture" would not differ from scientific knowledge as both are *social constructs* of the reality and are not objective representations of it. This way the author discards the "cognitivist presumption that risks or scientific knowledge exist independently as an object for measurable public attitudes or beliefs" (Wynne 1992, 300). Scientific knowledge is "as socially grounded [...] and value laden" as lay knowledge (Wynne 1992, 297).

Furthermore, the circumstance that in the Cumbrian case the scientific advice was even *incorrect* as based upon wrong scientific models (Wynne 1992, 286) not only demonstrates that a type of knowledge is never a priori better that the other but also challenges the "exaggerated sense of certainty and arrogance" (Wynne 1992, 287) which often surrounds scientific advice in controversial situations. In addition, the obsession of scientists with monitoring ("a proliferation of monitoring": Wynne 1992, 287) would conflict with the pretentious certainty of scientific statements. In the instance described by Wynne, the arrogant presumption of the scientists clashed with the nature of Cumbrian farmers' lay culture, where uncertainty was routinely accepted and a "flexible adaptation" was preferred over "prediction and control" (Wynne 1992, 287). That lay culture, framed by Wynne as an "expertise not codified anywhere [...] passed down orally and by apprenticeship from one generation to the next, as a craft tradition, reinforced in the culture of the area" (Wynne 1992, 295), could be assimilated to the special knowledge that local people have on the issues, which is key to citizen sensing (Boulos et al. 2011, 72).

These arguments show that lay knowledge is often not unreasonable; rather, in many cases it can be regarded as *specialist* knowledge, as valid as the scientific advice in the achievement of a solution to a risk problem. The analysis performed by Wynne suggests that the first step to reconcile this conflict between science and lay knowledge entails science's recognition of "its own conditionality" and bias (Wynne 1992, 297). Only this acknowledgement could lead to greater *legitimacy* and public uptake of science. Nevertheless, the author admits that for this major change to happen, institutional reforms are needed on the scientific "modes of organization, control and social relations". According to Wynne, for this transformation to happen it is necessary "inter alia, [science's] recognition of *new, socially extended peer groups legitimated* to offer criticism of scientific bodies of knowledge from *beyond the confines* of the immediate exclusive specialist scientific peer-group" [emphasis added] (Wynne 1992, 297). Particularly functional to this structural transformation are the "Lay criteria for judgment of science" (Wynne 1992, 298), listed by the author as follows [emphasis added]: "Does the scientific knowledge *work*? Do scientific claims *pay attention* to other available knowledge? Is the form of the knowledge as well as the content *recognisable*? Are scientists *open to criticism*? What are the social/institutional affiliations of experts? What issue 'overspill' exists in *lay experience*?" These questions are particularly relevant here.

I do not consider neither the scientific, nor the public (citizens), nor the political advice as the response to achieve the best risk governance possible (which, as I have argued before, does not even exist). Yet, I posit that the public advice (for example, through the channel of citizen sensing) *should* enter the debate on risk governance, and not only in the moment of tracking and assessing the risk but also in *defining* it. In the words of Power (2007, 16), the *legitimacy crisis* of expert knowledge calls for a better participation of lay public in the processes of risk framing and analysis and for an improved risk communication. Power's argument is here endorsed where I defend that citizens have a role to play not only in improving how risks are communicated, but also how they are governed. Adopting citizen sensing as a tool to complement expert input on risk from an early stage (but with the afore-discussed barriers to prevent unfounded claims) can stimulate a shared understanding on the risk at issue and promote a smoother governance thereof.

None of the three standpoints just mentioned—the scientific, the public or the political—is 'neutral', as each advice essentially contains values and norms which heavily shape how reality is seen by scientists, the public and policy-makers (Berti Suman 2018a). Bijker et al. (2009, 2, 16, 43) excellently showed how scientific facts have "interpretative flexibility" and that "scientific knowledge is always in flux" and not "a priori different from other types of knowledge". Rather, science is "made rather than found" and is "human handiwork", thus it could have been *otherwise* (Bijker et al. 2009, 29). Any action of assessing the external worlds is not 'pure' in the sense that it reflects not only the measured reality but also the *understanding* that the person has of it. For example, if a scientist, a layperson and a politician are asked to measure a problem that they perceive as a risk, although they measure it with the same tools, the results may be very different because decisions such as 'where the risk comes from', 'which individuals are at risk', 'which areas are more exposed to the risk' can vary substantially in accordance to different opinions and beliefs. As Bijker et al. (2009, 167) affirmed, "citizens, stakeholders, patients […] have all their own views […] and knowledge of this society with its science and technology. Democratic governance of technological cultures require that those forms of knowledge and experience are *recognized and allowed to play a role*" [emphasis added].

Also in the political arena, there has been debate on the question on how inclusive the process of risk knowledge production should be. The WHO acknowledged the role of a multi-stakeholder approach in the process of scientific knowledge *interpretation* in a report which reads as follows [emphasis added] (WHO 2013, 5):

> "By considering different perspectives and viewpoints, by collecting *informal pieces of evidence* and by comparing and contrasting preferences and needs, it is often possible to *interpret* scientific knowledge better [...] and to identify *more appropriate* and feasible policy options and improve their implementation. In other words, engaging directly in *open and evidence-informed dialogue on risks* [...] *improves the quality of the entire process.*"

Following this argument, citizen sensing could be seen as the 'informal piece of evidence' contributing to a better interpretation of scientific risk knowledge and to a more appropriate policy response to risks. While standing in favour of valorizing the layperson's contribution, yet I do not intend to challenge the legitimacy of the scientific and the political knowledge. I rather seek to *complement* them with the help that citizen sensing can offer with a view to coping with the challenges posed by risks that are every day more complex, uncertain and ambiguous.

Theory of Change: How Citizen Sensing Can Contribute to Risk Governance

In this section, a preliminary and abstract reflection on integration will be performed with the aim to verify how practices of citizen sensing may fit within current risk governance structures. The gaps and limitations of 'traditional' risk governance approaches have been discussed through the theoretical lens provided by the Millstone models. Now, I move to inspecting how such gaps and limitations can be addressed by means of a grassroots' contribution identified (also) in citizen sensing practices. More recent evolutions of traditional risk governance models are analysed as representing the most apt scenario for the insertion of citizen sensing in the system. Graphical illustrations of this integration will facilitate the discussion. An insight into the opinion of relevant experts with regard to the role of grassroots-produced knowledge in risk governance will complement the analysis.

To begin with, I postulate that, when an environmental health problem arises in a community, policy-makers should be able to reconcile the first-hand experience of residents with insights from scientists. Focusing exactly on environmental health policy-making, Corburn (2005) inspected how local knowledge can be combined with professional techniques to achieve stronger and more legitimate solutions to environmental health problems. For example, he studied the efforts of a low-income community located in Brooklyn in dealing with its environmental health problems. Corburn suggested a framework for understanding 'street science' that he frames as decision-making that draws on *community knowledge* and contributes to *environmental justice* (Corburn 2005). This pervasive potential of community knowledge suggests a theory of change.

The illustrated four 'classical' models of risk governance have undergone a process of reinterpretation in recent years. In the political arena, the IRGC in 2005 released an updated model of the risk governance process (IRGC 2005). The model is contained in a White Paper titled "Risk Governance: Towards an *Integrative* Approach" [emphasis added]. The integration of multiple stakeholders in risk governance is perceived as essential, which is a progress particularly noteworthy for the aims of this research. According to the model, the structure of risk governance is articulated in four phases: pre-assessment, appraisal, characterization and evaluation, and risk management (Renn et al. 2011, 236). According to the analysis provided by Renn et al. (2011, 236), the two key elements shaping all the process are *communication* and *stakeholder involvement*. This consideration is extremely timely to this research because practices of citizen sensing often arise from communication deficits and bring the promise to stimulate a horizontal and open communication about risks. Moreover, a prerequisite of citizen sensing is exactly (lay) stakeholders' involvement.

However, the question on *which stakeholders* and *how* to involve them is not clearly answered in the model proposed by the IRGC. This is understandable as, in the end, these choices are extremely contextual to the risk at issue and the situation in which such a risk is inserted (Renn et al. 2011, 236). Although formalized models such as those proposed by the IRGC seem too 'static' for capturing the multitude of actors and of relationships characterizing risk governance, yet it seems worth to explore *whether and where* citizen sensing could fit in these established models. This effort of integration and the related graphical representations may oversimplify the complex dynamics underlying the integration of grassroots knowledge in current risk governance structures. However, as long as these images are considered non-exhaustive and static representations of the reality, they may still help understanding the sought integration. To this aim, the IRGC Risk Governance Process (IRGC 2005, 65) has been edited to indicate in which phases of the process citizen sensing could play a role (in Fig. 4.1, they are circled in red). In particular, I deem that citizen sensing may contribute to the 'Pre-Assessment' (quoted from the IRGC's model, IRGC 2005, 65) of the risk problem and specifically to 'early warning' on the risk. In addition, I posit that the practice could contribute to the 'Risk Appraisal' phase by bringing in data about 'Risk Perceptions' and 'Social Concerns'. Lastly, citizen sensing could improve risk management by facilitating 'Monitoring and Control' interventions. Overall, citizen sensing might also enhance and support Risk Communication as indicated above. This potential contribution, here hypothesized only in theory and at a very preliminary stage of the research, should be verified in the practice of the empirical reality.

Renn et al. (2011, 237) proposed a number of modifications to the IRGC model presenting a new risk governance sequence based on pre-estimation, interdisciplinary risk estimation, risk characterization, risk evaluation and risk management. Although it is impossible to dive into the details of each phase (which can be found in Renn et al. 2011, 238–243) here, it is useful to reflect on what guided the authors in performing this reformulation. They justified the changes under the argument that effective risk governance "requires the ability and capacity of risk governance institutions to use *resources* effectively" [emphasis added]. Among these resources, 'Social Capital' is listed, which—I argue—also includes grassroots' knowledge. The term 'resources' indeed refers also to human resources, such as epistemic communities. Moreover, the authors refer to

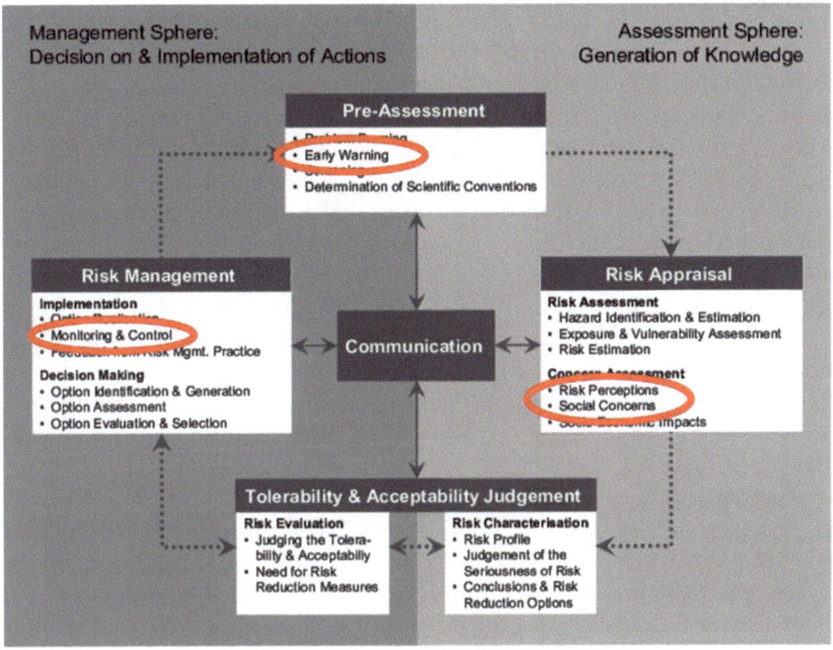

Fig. 4.1 Citizen sensing 'fit' in the IRGC Risk Governance Process (IRGC 2005, 65)

"formal and *informal* networks that promote collective risk handling and education" (Renn et al. 2011, 237).

The idea of a collective handling of risk by reliance on social capital recalls the work of Ostrom (1996, 1073) and her theory of Co-Production. Ostrom defines 'co-production' as "the process through which inputs used to produce a good or service are contributed by individuals who are not 'in' the same organization". Co-production resonates with broader notions of public dialogue and of public engagement (Irwin et al. 2013), yet being very different from multiple stakeholders' involvement in decision-making. Rather, the concept focuses the attention on how the knowledge on which decisions are made is essentially the result of a multifaceted interaction of epistemologies, spanning from scientific to civic forms of knowledge.

Recently, Brandsen and Honingh (2016) revisited the concept and provided a categorization of the different types of co-production to clarify the meaning of Ostrom's—in their opinion, fuzzy—concept. The authors focused on identifying different regimes for knowledge (co-) production, different temporalities, different kinds of knowledge etc. Other authors, using the 'ecology metaphor', analysed co-production as a diverse *ecosystem* (Chilvers and Kearnes 2015, 13). The authors suggest that co-production, through the inclusion of different forms of knowledge, generates a sense of responsibility and thus leads to new *geographies* of responsibility, an aspect which appeared particularly evident also in my empirical data. As a matter of fact, new geographies of responsibility may indicate a new allocation of responsibilities among the actors that interplay on the governance arena. This new allocation may respond to a demand from the (sensing) citizens to be listened by risk governors in their decisions.

Jasanoff (2004)—as interpreted by Bijker et al. (2009, 5)—discusses the 'co-production of science and society', referring to the intertwined development of scientific knowledge and social order. Citizen science can be regarded as an excellent example of this intertwined development as the scientific knowledge produced through these practices is inherently embedded with '*civic epistemologies*'. Jasanoff defines these epistemologies as "the institutionalized practices by which members of a given society test and deploy knowledge claims used as a basis for making *collective choices*" [emphasis added] (Jasanoff 2005). Actually, all scientific processes of knowledge-making as well as policy decisions based on such processes are, to different degrees, shaped by and embedded in civic epistemologies. In addition, Jasanoff and Kim (2013) argue that attention should also be devoted to 'co-imagination', framed as collectively defining 'socio-technical imaginaries' which embody collective desires and emotions. Citizen sensing within this frame would be a civic epistemology presenting *new imaginaries* that potentially could form (part of) the basis for *orienting collective choices*.

The lens of co-production developed by Jasanoff has been readapted and applied to a multitude of sectors. For example, Glesner and Van Oudheusden[1] inspect the construction of safety and security cultures—in particular in the context of critical infrastructures such as nuclear power

[1] Presentation delivered during the conference that I attended: "TILTing Perspectives 2019: Regulating a World in Transition", Tilburg, The Netherlands, May 15–17, 2019.

plants—through the lens of co-production. The authors reflect on how these two cultures mutually inform and shape each other and incorporate similarly technological, procedural and human aspects. They also look at how concepts of vulnerability and resilience apply to the two cultures, investigating how more or less explicit tensions among actors interplay both in safety and in security cultures. From the co-production theoretical endeavour, Glesner and Van Oudheusden suggest an integrated model of safety and security cultures that they contextualize through empirical research within the field of critical infrastructures.

Co-production theory is also applied here to the different but somehow adjacent field of citizen sensing. Figure 1 in Klinke and Renn (2011, Figure 1),[2] offers a risk governance framework. In particular, the phases of "Monitoring and Control" and of "Communication, Deliberation and Involvement" of this framework as well as the "Human Resources and Social Capital" are dimensions in which citizen sensing could play an important role, contributing to risk governance. Indeed, as noted when discussing the IRGC's model (Fig. 4.1), I posit that citizen sensing could fit the monitoring and control phase and distinctive aspects of the communication and public engagement phases, which are crucial for assessing risk perceptions and social concerns (these dimensions are parts of the "Risk Appraisal" in Fig. 4.1 cited). In addition, the "Human Resources" and "Social Capital" components of Klinke and Renn's risk governance framework[3] are relevant as citizen sensing may contribute to strengthening these resources.

What is particularly endorsed from this framework is the acknowledgement that risk evaluation and governance should be a multi-dimensional process. Renn et al. (2011, 240) argue that risk evaluation starts with an activity aimed at characterizing the risks on "all the dimensions that matter to the affected populations". In addition, the authors stress the role of moral considerations in the evaluation of risks by affirming: "the question of what is safe enough implies a moral judgment about acceptability of risk and the tolerable burden that risk producers can impose on others" (Renn et al. 2011, 240). The importance of risk perception and

[2] The original figure of the cited risk governance framework can be found as Figure 1 in Klinke and Renn, 2011, at https://doi.org/10.1080/13669877.2011.63683.

[3] Ibid.

risk acceptability, and the attention to the affected populations particularly resonate with the aims of my study. Especially with regards to risk acceptability, the idea of a social compromise emerges, implied in the idea of 'tolerable burden'. Whereas, in an ideal world, environmental risks to public health should be *completely* removed, it is pertinent to argue that a balance between the interests of economic growth that may lead to environmental risks and optimal public and environmental health conditions should be found.

Although I stressed the importance of the integration of *all* affected stakeholders in risk governance processes, it is still worth wondering to whom belongs the ultimate responsibility for how the risk is governed, question which is "too often overlooked by participation oriented approaches" (Renn et al. 2011, 241, citing Garrelts and Lange 2011). Monitoring and governing (environmental) risk ultimately is a responsibility of the State or is it rather a matter of a *collective responsibility*? If the ultimate responsibility is considered as *always* on the State, "a reverse movement from governance to government" would take place (Renn et al. 2011, 241). Bijker et al. (2009, 167) stressed that the ultimate responsibility to take a decision over a risk is on a "democratically checked government". Yet, "the decision is best made at the end of a process involving a variety of parties". I argue (in line with Renn et al. 2011, 242; and Bijker et al. 2009) that for low ambiguity/low uncertainty risk, regardless of their complexity, a 'government' (*alias* non-participatory) approach may be preferable because it is often more time- and cost-effective. Differently, for highly ambiguous and uncertain risks, participative processes and multi-level stakeholders' engagement are advisable.

This resonates with the conclusion of Bijker et al. (2009, 162, 164), who defended that in case of simple risk situations, routine risk management techniques can be used without the need to involve external stakeholders. Complex situations could be tackled by involving more scientists from a broader spectrum (but still internally to the scientists' groups). In case of uncertain and ambiguous risks, participatory process would instead be indispensable (Bijker et al. 2009, 162, 164). I endorse this distinction, supporting the value of citizens' input especially in case of uncertain and ambiguous risk problems. As stressed above, this does not mean overturning the system but rather striving for a *shared responsibility* over the risk.

Relevant literature (for example, Boholm et al. 2012) has criticized risk governance models, such as the IRGC framework, for being too generic and formalized, advocating instead for a contextual and practice-based approach. More than being captured by abstract models, risk governance would be about "solving actual problems through routines, *trust*, mutual understanding and not least, *shared commitment* to the societal role of infrastructure" [emphasis added] (Boholm et al. 2012, 1). The said authors (2012, 1) suggest that "risk governance takes place in contexts that are historically, spatially and institutionally situated" and, consequently, risk governance practices should be analysed by focusing on "the characteristics of this contextuality" rather than by trying to crystallize them in general models. I deem that the actualization proposed by Renn et al. (2011, 237) to the IRGC's model already goes in that direction, bringing more contextuality into the IRGC's model and adding societal nuances to it. In order to contribute to this effort to go beyond formalized and static models, I decided to interview three experts on risk governance and related subjects, through semi-structured, in-person interviews. An expert of Risk Governance and an expert of Citizen Science[4] from RIVM have been interviewed. In addition, an expert of Responsible Innovation and of Urban Innovation theories from Delft University of Technology has been consulted.[5]

The expert of Risk Governance at RIVM confirmed the existence of predominant 'approaches' to risk governance, in spite of the impossibility to identify *a* dominant model. The interviewee noted that the prevailing institutional patterns of risk governance are often based on a vertical control over the risk monitoring system; a denial of discussion over the appropriateness of this approach; and an insufficiently adaptive and integrative system. The expert endorsed the inclusion of practices entailing citizen participation in risk governance such as citizen sensing. However, the interviewee stressed the importance of taking into account *the culture* of the community where the risk is inserted, in order for a proper integration to happen. Indeed, the success or failure of the integration of citizen

[4] Interviews performed on June 26, 2017, at RIVM, Bilthoven, The Netherlands. Recorded with permission and later transcribed.

[5] Interview performed on May 31, 2017, at Delft University of Technology, Delft, The Netherlands.

sensing into an institutional system of risk governance may be highly influenced by social and cultural factors as, in the end, risk is essentially a social construct.

Particularly noteworthy is the answer of the expert when confronted with the direct question: "Do you think the prevailing models of risk governance should go through a structural process of regeneration?" The interviewee answered that this process was *already* ongoing. The expert identified the demarcation line of this gradual shift towards a more participatory approach to risk governance "somewhere in the 90's". The expert acknowledged the role of the above-mentioned Red Book (1983) and of the subsequent recognition in the '90s by the U.S. National Research Council of the interrelation between the risk assessment and the risk management phases. The expert also mentioned the importance of the IRGC in the process of transforming risk governance. The interviewee stressed that "risk governance is also about *engaging stakeholders* and about the quality of the engagement etc. [...] For simple problems, you can leave the risk assessment to technical people, but if it is getting more complex, uncertain and ambiguous, you need to *engage much more in the stakeholder dialogue*" [emphasis added], confirming what I have argued here. The expert concluded reaffirming that "the end of the '90's, early 2000, is about the tipping point that people started to appreciate that [...] *risk is more than a number*. So that is about where I would put the demarcation line" [emphasis added].

The interviewed expert of Citizen Science at RIVM added other relevant points. First, the interviewee stressed that, regardless the successful integration of citizen sensing in institutional models, the only fact that lay people start monitoring has an impact in itself as it challenges the assumption that the institutional and prevailing approach is valid. According to the expert, the clash of methods for risk measurement and governance would be already constructive and necessary to extrapolate the truth from each argument, and to improve the functioning of the system (as I also noted in Berti Suman 2018a). "I wonder if it is really so bad if there is an open conflict about the data", said the interviewee. In the words of Bijker et al. (2009, 103) this positive "scepticism, confrontation and debate" could be framed as 'creative dissent' which can actually contribute to the achievement of a 'serviceable truth', i.e., "knowledge that can stand the scientific test of criticism". Despite recognizing here the *constructive* role of the conflict, I acknowledge that conflict can also lead to failures in the system and sub-optimal results, such as loss of resources. The

Fig. 4.2 Clash and convergence of citizen sensing in the current models of risk governance (Berti Suman 2018b, 269)

(arguably positive) clash and, eventually, subsequent integration (considered a 'success' for the initiative and the institution) of citizen sensing into institutional risk governance is illustrated in Fig. 4.2.

Later in the interview, the expert captured the grassroots' nature of citizen sensing by differentiating it from more institutionalized citizen science practices performed by lay people but coordinated by scientists. Conversely, in their opinion, citizen sensing "could fall under the extreme citizen science group, where people say 'well, we do not believe that the air quality is good so we will do our own measurements'". Lastly, the expert stressed that "sensing alone is not enough, you also need to analyse the data. And you need to translate the analysis into knowledge. *Data is not knowledge, knowledge is not yet wisdom.* Much more needs to be done than the sensing only" [emphasis added]. This argument reminds the importance of making *wise use* of the sensed data, from which I derive the need of inspecting the policy uptake of citizen sensing (Berti Suman 2021), to avoid that the practice rests a void amatorial act. Moreover, from the interview, it emerged the importance of integrating citizen sensing not only in the data collection phase of risk governance, but also in the data analysis stage and in the implementation of measures on the basis of the collected data.

Finally, it is worth stressing that in the integration of grassroots practices into institutional models, tools and data's ownership questions should be addressed as they ultimately reflect power structures. The interviewee from Delft University of Technology wondered under this aspect: "who owns and governs the risk measuring sensors and the results?" (related reflections in Berti Suman 2018a). In an integrative approach, the sensing citizens should be able to have control on both the sensors and the outcomes of their measurements, in spite of the policy uptake of the initiative. However, for the integration to work, this measuring system should be *trusted* and recognized as valid at the institutional level. In line with this discussion, I proposed earlier that the reliance on 'community standards' can facilitate the acceptance of citizen sensing by institutional actors and scientists (see Berti Suman 2019a). Also the need to balance ownership and openness of the tools and of the relative results seems pressing, as well as the importance to consider data protection issues while supporting openness (as I inspected in Berti Suman and Pierce 2018), in order to ensure that risk governors can regard the citizen sensing projects as legally sound.

Lastly, the interviewed expert pointed out that that the *status quo* (vertical governance of the risk in which institutional actors control the measuring tools and the relative data produced, and define the parameters to be measured) may not change until 'a break' occurs (as I stressed also in Berti Suman 2018a). The turning point identified by the interviewee may coincide with the rise of unexpected and alternative or complementary risk measurement systems falling under the umbrella of citizen sensing practices, which at the beginning *destabilize* the system and later can contribute to its improvement (Berti Suman 2018b).

Theoretical Justifications for Including Citizen Sensing in Institutional Risk Governance

In this book, citizen sensing has been presented as potentially a method for contributing to risk governance, intended as encompassing the assessment of a risk as well as the search and implementation of solutions to a given risk problem. The underlying assumption is that the sensing citizens, besides contributing to produce data over risks, have *a key role* to play in defining the responses that are currently predominantly decided by scientists and policy-makers. Throughout my empirical analysis, I will assess whether and under which conditions this role subsists.

In a study recently released (Hicks et al. 2019, 1), the "huge promise" of broader citizen science for Disaster Risk Reduction (DRR) was demonstrated through a systematic global mapping of citizen science initiatives used for DRR. The authors analysed 106 examples of citizen science applied to DRR over the world and inspected the actual relevance of these projects for supporting risk reduction. Paul et al. (2018, 1), also referring to risk citizen science but in the specific context of hydrological risk, argued that the practice is playing an "emerging" role in Disaster Risk Management (DRM). Discussing examples from flood response and drought alleviation, the authors—despite acknowledging that "non-scientist local stakeholders have *always* played an important role in knowledge risk management and resilience building"—note that "a 'citizen science' approach has recently emerged as a *promising direction* in the provision of an extensive, *real-time information for risk management*" [emphasis added] (Paul et al. 2018, 1). Strongly in line with my argument, Paul et al. (2018, 1) stressed that citizen science, especially when "embedded within a *polycentric approach toward risk governance*, […] could complement more traditional knowledge generation practices, and also enhance […] adaptation, multidirectional information provision, risk management, and local resilience building" [emphasis added]. This push for a more 'polycentric' risk governance, as also illustrated by the revisions proposed to the IRGC models, could create a fertile ground for *complementing* traditional risk governance with citizen sensing. Yet, institutional actors may struggle to accept this input from the grassroots (Berti Suman 2019b). Thus, it is worth exploring which grounds could make citizen sensing practices *legitimate* in the eyes of policy-makers (as discussed by Berti Suman et al. 2020) and scientists, starting from a socio-political and STS-oriented analysis.

A first source of legitimacy can be found in the actual contributing and complementary potential of citizen sensing. As argued by Becker et al. (2013, 1), there would be a "cross-fertilization process" between practices of participatory sensing and institutional risk monitoring. The two approaches can mutually improve each other, as illustrated in Fig. 4.3. The authors gathered empirical insights from the case of grassroots noise monitoring and concluded that the citizen-reported (objective and subjective) noise data represent a substantial opportunity for tackling noise pollution. Basing risk governance decisions on wider empirical grounds which also include lay knowledge could help achieving 'evidence-based' policies (Teisman and Klijn 2008). In addition, citizen sensing could be a way to make science more effective in cases of "post-normal science" (Funtowicz and Ravetz 1993, 750) i.e., in tackling issues which, due to their complexity and singularity, demand inclusive problem-solving approaches (Bäckstrand 2003, 30–35).

Furthermore, the growing uncertain nature of the risks that science must currently handle suggests that "technologies of hubris" (predictive risk governance methods that facilitate control by oversimplifying issues and claiming objectivity) should be refused, and "technologies of humility" that acknowledge the limits of prediction and control and foresee citizen engagement in science should rather be adopted (Jasanoff 2003). The 'deficit model', according to which laypersons would be scientifically illiterate and ignorant, is rejected and the role of "local, subjugated knowledge" is conversely defended (Bäckstrand 2003, 30). Nonetheless, it has been argued that it is still unproven whether political and social issues (thus including environmental and public health issues) are better addressed through exclusive reliance on technical expertise or rather through citizen participation and democratic deliberation (Bäckstrand 2003, 24). The question on whether citizen input should be included in the production, validation and application of science is *unresolved* because the "theoretical foundations for coupling democratic citizen participation with scientific assessment" are still missing (Bäckstrand 2003, 27). This book strives to contribute to this gap.

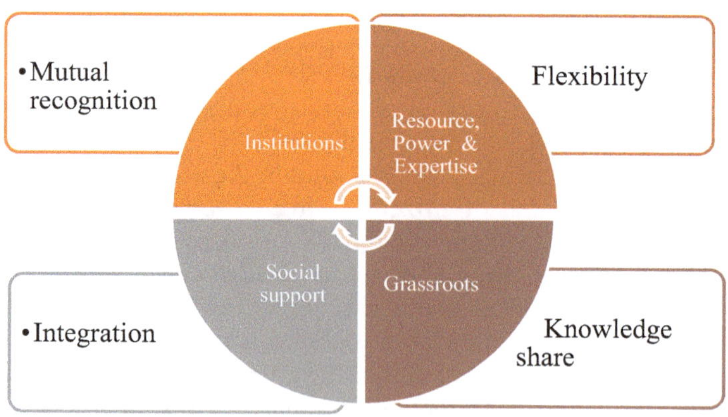

Fig. 4.3 Mutual contribution between grassroots and institutional risk governance

A second source of legitimacy for allowing citizen sensing in risk governance could derive from the acknowledgement that experts and laypersons are no longer two strictly distinct categories. In a society where what counts as "credible, authoritative and legitimate expert knowledge is increasingly blurred" (Bäckstrand 2003, 27), the need to recognize forms of expertise in citizen sensing practices seems pressing. These forms of expertise could be framed as 'contro-expertise' as often opposing prevailing expert knowledge. They indeed provide alternative discourses to the prevailing ones and support claims of affected citizens and environmental activists against the institutional way of handling a specific risk. In the end, these groups need to 'mobilize' science and ground their arguments with data (the 'citizen-sensed' data) if they want to challenge the institutional risk governance system and ultimately be listened by policy-makers.

I also stressed in this book that citizen sensing not only engages laypersons. Among the sensing citizens, there may also be experts just not acting in their role of experts, which demonstrates that the divide between citizens and experts is not straightforward. Bijker et al. (2009, 25, 30) joined the claim for a fluid distinction between experts and laypersons, pointing that there are forms of expertise [...] which no one would call scientific, but which nonetheless provide a *valuable complement to scientific expertise*" [emphasis added]. STS scholarship has largely demonstrated that citizens' understanding of scientific and technological issues "could be much more valid and relevant than generally assumed" (Bijker et al. 2009, 153; Wynne 1982). Wynne (1982) focusing on the controversy surrounding the Windscale nuclear fuel facility and the Cumbrian farmers concluded that lay judgements 'deviating' from the established scientific opinion should be understood as the result of a different framing and perception of the issue, rather than as signs of irrationality or ignorance. The argument that citizen sensing cannot contribute to risk governance because it lacks the necessary expertise can be easily discarded. What is instead defendable is that there may be a conflict between the institutional and grassroots' way of perceiving and assessing risks, although there is no agreement on what counts as institutional and what as grassroots. In fact, Bäckstrand (2003, 25), when discussing the "triangular interaction between scientific experts, policy-makers and citizen [scientists]", does not define how to distinguish the categories and whether such strict categories are sound.

Furthermore, citizen sensing could find legitimacy also as a response to the growing complexity of current (environmental) issues demanding for a more polycentric management of risks, as noted above. Luhmann (1993, 527), in his notorious article "Ecological communication: Coping with the unknown", unveils a growing concern towards how science and modern society cope with complex problems. The author shows scepticism towards traditional processes of rational decision-making, societal ability to plan, and human's "cognitive capacity for prediction and directing action" (Luhmann 1993, 527). For Luhmann, "the way forward is to recognize the increasing uncertainties" (1993, 527) society faces and do so as *a collective process* of awareness. Nonetheless, the author concludes his piece with a very triggering question: "How can we cope with the unknown?" (Luhmann 1993, 539). Citizen sensing in this book is not presented as 'the solution'. Not at all. Yet, it can help bringing in the civic perspective, both in cases of deep uncertainties, such as the real health consequences of an environmental contaminant, and in the response to unexpected events, such as the Fukushima disaster.

Lastly, citizen sensing could be presented and thus justified as *a response to the legitimacy crisis of science*, described by Bijker et al. (2009). The said authors (2009, 2) pose a timely question: "How can we understand the authority of science while recognizing its socially constructed nature?" It could be argued that citizen science and sensing are aimed at contesting official science. Citizen sensing sometimes aims at resisting institutional science. However, I also defend that, even if through an (eventual) conflict stage, participatory forms of scientific knowledge production could be a way to make science (and in particular scientific evidence for political decision-making) more open to the interested public(s) in a moment of 'crisis' of scientific authority. Participation in and contribution to the process and understanding of how this process works may, eventually, contribute to restore public trust in science (Bäckstrand 2003, 30–35) and, arguably, also in policy-making based on scientific facts. Citizen sensing can contribute to the *democratization* of science, considering democracy in its 'strong' sense, that is, not only representative but also participatory democracy (Bäckstrand 2003). Ezrahi (2012) too reflected on the connection between participatory knowledge and democracy, affirming that the inclusion of people in policy-making through knowledge is an *aspiration* of democratic societies.

As advocated by Bijker et al. (2009, 2) there is a compelling need to inspect "possible *new roles* for scientists and *citizens* in technological democracies" [emphasis added]. The authors acknowledged the already complementary potential played by the citizens' input in addressing scientific problems when they demand: "How can scientific advice still play a role in the democratic governance of technological cultures, where *participation by citizens* [...] increasingly complements the old institutional mechanisms of democracy?" [emphasis added]. The plea for public involvement in science and technology is way older, dating back to the reflections of Dewey (1927) and Ezrahi (1990) who inspired STS scholarship on the analysis of the interplay between science, technology and democracy (Bijker et al. 2009, 3). Despite supporting such a plea, Bijker et al. (2009, 46, 165) criticized the democratization of scientific advisory bodies such as the Health Council of the Netherlands, arguing that, if all deliberations would become public and the members of these bodies would start representing various interest groups, the needed independency of scientific advice could be harmed and its quality ultimately undermined.

Reflections on the role of lay knowledge in traditionally expert-based sectors are currently flourishing in the academic, political and scientific debates. I could dive into similar discussions during the conference "Unpacking the 'Accountability Paradox' in Expert-Based Decision-making".[6] Among the relevant concerns brought to the fore, the contamination between *public* and private science (e.g., the increasingly encouraged partnerships between industry and academia) was discussed, as alimenting claims for a 'disinterested' science. A controversial arena emerged where 'independent' science is opposed to 'biased' science, which would not reflect public interests, such as health and environmental protection. Discussants stressed issues such as the claimed lack of scientific independence, the strategic use of uncertainty, science as a source of power, accountability gaps and 'revolving doors' phenomena. This misperception of science seems worsening every day, also as a consequence of the release of documents fomenting public distrust. Experience of scandals such as the mentioned Glyphosate Saga and the Monsanto Papers contributed to this sense of distrust, which indeed heavily depends on past experience and on history. Citizen sensing seems alimented by these experiences that generated societal distrust.

[6] Conference "Unpacking the 'Accountability Paradox' in Expert-Based Decision-making", which I attended, at the Erasmus School of Law, Erasmus University of Rotterdam, Rotterdam, The Netherlands, December 1, 2017.

Within this context, citizen sensing not only aims at finding facts but also at assessing compliance of policy decisions with norms and citizens' expectations. Such policy decisions, as stressed earlier, are often based on science, especially in the field of environmental risks, which in turn is not at all 'values-free' (Douglas 2009), position that highly resonates with the praise developed here for embracing citizen science and sensing, albeit imbued with (participants') values. Values are *essential* in such decisional processes because they can shape judgements on risk acceptability and determine how serious the consequences of making the wrong decision would be. Values can orient the act of balancing the risk of a wrong decision with the interests to be protected, and the decision on what should prevail in this balancing. Citizen science and sensing embed values too, and to a high level. But values are different from interests: value-based science can still be 'disinterested'. It is unavoidable that science generated in a specific historical period and geographical area will embed social norms inherent to that specific time and context However, the discussion here revolves around *whose* norms, values and interests are allowed to shape science and to ground 'science-based' decisions. The very question then is how to make this reliance on certain values transparent and explicit to the public? And how to ensure that also grassroots' actors can inject values in the system? Lastly, how can society exercise an oversight on the correct transposition of values in science and policies? Substantial and external, rather than only procedural and internal, accountability mechanisms could arguably help in avoiding 'black box' science, making the grounding of policy decisions into science a more transparent process to the public(s).

This approach needs to go beyond solely expert-based risk governance and to investigate a complementary approach based on citizen sensing can be regarded as part of what Giddens (1990) discussed as the 'transition between traditional (pre-modern) culture and post-traditional (modern) culture' (Berti Suman 2018b). Giddens describes this transition as the shift from the reliance on the 'wise' elderly in pre-modern societies who were granted the trust of the community, to modern societies where a sense of uncertainty and *delegitimization* of experts' decisions (who became the new 'wise men') dominates. As Jasanoff (1987) earlier argued, the legitimacy of decision-makers in a specific community ultimately depends upon their ability to reconstruct a 'plausible scientific rationale for the proposed action'. The plausibility of this rationale also depends on the trust that people have in those decision-makers.

The outlined transition can be also inserted in the 'structural transformation of the public sphere' discussed by Habermas (1991). Within this structural transformation, *new publics*, here identified as the sensing citizens, take responsibility for risks affecting them, challenging the understanding of the State as the sole governor thereof. Mahlouly (2013) brought forward Habermas' theory on the transformation of the public space, taking the perspective of today's *virtual* public spaces. The author identified a number of parallelisms between the Eighteenth-Century society described by Habermas and the present times. In particular, Mahlouly (2013) inspects the potential of '*connective culture(s)*' to make people conscious of their political power and to promote a democratic culture stimulated by forms of online activism. However, Mahlouly (2013, 18) notes also that "it is not clear to what extent this form of political engagement is sustainable in the context of a representative democracy". This question will be inspected building on previous reflections on the feasibility of participatory approaches to risk governance in democratic societies.[7]

When discussing the legitimacy of citizen sensing in institutional settings, it should be noted that recently there has been a growing acknowledgement of the value of a proactive citizen engagement in science and policy-making. At the EU level, in particular the European Commission Joint Research Center (JRC) has often advocated for such an engagement. Here the stance of the JRC specifically in regard to the role of lay people in current (risk) policy-making is illustrated. In the JRC Science for Policy Report "Citizen Engagement in Science and Policy-Making" (Figueiredo Nascimento et al. 2016), the EC welcomes citizen-driven contributions to science and policy also over risks. It is affirmed that citizen engagement, especially in heavily 'expert-based' sectors, can bring about "democratic *legitimacy, accountability and transparent* governance" [emphasis added] (Figueiredo Nascimento et al. 2016, 3). Furthermore, the potential of citizen involvement for enhancing "*trust* building among citizens and institutions as well as *ownership of*

[7] In Berti Suman (2018b), I explored this discussion drawing a 'taxonomy' on the complementary potential of citizen sensing in respect to public-health risk governance in the (smart) city, building on the theory of the complexity of society (Castells 1996), through its reinterpretation given by Fisher (2017). The research contained in this book partially takes inspiration from these arguments but leaves aside the (smart) city scenario.

policy outcome" [emphasis added] is stressed (Figueiredo Nascimento et al. 2016, 3).

The recent interest of the EU institutions and in particular of the JRC towards citizen science and sensing as a form of laypersons' engagement in (risk) science and policy has not been flanked by a similar attention from academics active on topics related to risk governance. A search within the journals such as the "European Journal of Risk Regulation" or the "Journal of Risk and Uncertainty" has not delivered articles related to the potential of citizen sensing for risk governance. In 2019, the Journal of Risk Research has published an article on the topic titled "The role of information in multilateral governance of environmental health risk: lessons from the Equatorial Asian Haze case" (Berti Suman 2019b). Later, in 2023, the Journal of Open Access to Law featured an article on "Citizen-gathered data to support public services under emergencies: promises and perils of openness" (Berti Suman 2023). Greater attention towards the subject is instead shown by more technology-oriented journals, as the "Journal of Sensors", the "GeoJournal", "Information, Communication & Society" and "Big Data & Society", or hard sciences and sectorial journals such as the mentioned study from Hicks et al. (2019) in "Frontiers in Earth Science". This book aims at contributing to fill this gap in the literature.

Case Insight 3: Making Risk Governance More Horizontal

Risk Governance Through Citizen Sensing

Faced with extreme weather events, more and more local administrations are turning to citizen sensing to co-govern shared risks. Over the past two years, I reviewed existing experiences where lay people have been successfully engaged in data collection over climate-induced risks. A good starting point is to look at existing flood risk citizen observatories, such as the Civic Observatory of the Brenta Bacchiglione Catchment,[8] created in the context of the WeObserve project[9] and hosted by the

[8] For a study on the initiative, see https://hess.copernicus.org/articles/24/5781/2020/.

[9] See https://www.weobserve.eu/.

Italian Eastern Alps Hydrographic District.[10] In the Observatory, local people are engaged in reporting floods occurrences data in order to help authorities in the early-warning phase, thus mitigating social vulnerability to flood risk. An exploratory inquiry is ongoing to assess distinctive and successful instances like this that signal a structural inclusion of citizen sensing in official risk governance patterns, especially starting from the local level.

A Shared Burden of Making the Risk (More) Visible

Connected to the overarching theme of making risk governance more horizontal, the idea of a shared responsibility for managing risks emerged. An unnamed project's volunteer stated that "responsible for coping [with the risk] are government (regulations) [and] citizens (personal changes)" [only square brackets added by me]. PurpleAir volunteers noted that responsible for the risk are "all levels of government; business managers; consumers." Safecast's participants too referred to "citizens and governments" and also to "TEPCO [i.e., Tokyo Electric Power Company, the Japanese company operating the Fukushima Daiichi plant], the IAEA [i.e., the International Atomic Energy Agency], the Japanese and local governments". For an I-REACT participant, "governments are responsible for protecting their citizens, but *citizens are also responsible for their own safety.* Our engagement tools aim to educate citizens but also to communicate with them in times of emergency by sharing timely information with them and *also receiving on-the spot reports from them.*" The aspect of the citizen as a proactive source of risk information seems crucial in this response: "we [i.e., I-REACT] use *data inputs from various sources including citizens* through the use of social media. This means that [...] we are also receiving further information from the general public."

Citizen Sensing for Everyone

In the analysis of the responses from the volunteers of citizen sensing initiatives to exploratory and targeted surveys, I noted a recurrence of the word 'everybody'/ 'everyone'. A voice from Safecast, for example, stressed "*Everyone* can upload their data. No one is forced to measure somewhere else; *everyone* can measure where and what they want. Also, the API is open source, and *everyone* can download the data and use it

[10] See https://www.weobserve.eu/autorita-di-bacino-dei-fiumi-isonzo-tagliamento-livenza-piave-brenta-bacchiglione-aawa/.

for research. Also these data are accessible for *everyone.*" Indeed "volunteers decide [what, how and when to measure] by participating in *open* joint discussions." This suggests the potential of the initiative to open radiation's risk governance to 'every citizen' (although citizen sensing is not always that 'open' and accessible to everybody). In spite of this 'grassroots-drive', a respondent noted that Safecast is proud to see that their "measurement methods have become [...] standards for some". A participant stressed also the 'everywhere' component: "Put into the public domain, [our data are] shared online everywhere." Understanding seems a necessary first step to then take action. Through Safecast, "it's easy to *understand* and to look up for *everyone.* They are doing workshops every now and then to get a *better understanding* about radiation. I visited these workshops, and they are *really informative.*" A volunteer even thinks that "[they] give the power to collect and explain the data on radiation to the *general public*". For another volunteer, it is enough to make the data publicly available, without engaging in steering people. "Public debate is left to the public."

Learning While Monitoring

The sensing initiatives are addressed to and welcome participants from both those citizens exposed to a risk and those who just want to support, despite not being affected. Yet, the distinction emerged from the volunteers' discourse. A Safecast participant acknowledged the learning rather than life-saving benefit from Safecast: "Until now, radiation *didn't had any effects on my life.* Only that this topic got a little bit more popular in [my country] in 2011, after the Fukushima Daiichi meltdown. But through Safecast, I *learned* a lot about radiation." Differently, for those directly affected by the disaster, "Safecast successfully provided both information and tool to measure radiation. These are *what those who have been exposed to the radiation really wanted*". PurpleAir volunteers connected the initiative to personal experiences of ailments associated with poor environmental conditions. One volunteer—who discovered about the project "by a local attorney who is *dying of a lung disorder*"—said: "My mother *suffered and died* from lung problems; I am sensitive to PM 2.5."

Seriously Concerned Citizens

Regardless being or not actually exposed, most respondents had a worried stance towards the issue: "Measure to avoid danger, search in order to know the safety." Interestingly, almost all respondents to my targeted survey, to the question "How serious do you think the problem(s) is/are on a 0–10 scale (0 meaning the lowest, 10 the highest)?" and "How concerned are you with regards to this/these problem(s) on a 0–10 scale (0 meaning the lowest, 10 the highest)?" answered always "10" (from air quality, to nuclear radiation after Fukushima). This seems to suggest that either they were *all* extremely concerned with the issue and considered it objectively serious at the highest level, or they ***did not perceive the variations*** in risk seriousness, as—for them—the problem they were dealing with was always of outmost seriousness and concern.

References

Bäckstrand, K. 2004. "Citizen science for sustainability: Reframing the role of experts, policy-makers and citizens in environmental governance." *Global Environmental Politics* 3 (4): 24–41. https://doi.org/10.1162/152638003322757916.

Becker, M., S. Caminiti, D. Fiorella, D., L. Francis, P. Gravino, M. Haklay, A. Hotho, et al. 2013. "Awareness and learning in participatory noise sensing". *Plos One* 8 (12): 1–12. https://doi.org/10.1371/journal.pone.0081638.

Berti Suman, A. 2018a. "Challenging risk governance patterns through citizen sensing: the Schiphol Airport case". *International Review of Law, Computers & Technology* 32 (1). https://doi.org/10.1080/13600869.2018.1429186.

Berti Suman, A. 2018b. "The smart transition: An opportunity for a sensor-based public-health risk governance?" *International Review of Law, Computers & Technology* 32 (2–3), *Special issue on 'Smart Cities or Smart Machines: Data Infrastructures and the Rule(s) of Law'*: 257–274. https://doi.org/10.1080/13600869.2018.1463961.

Berti Suman, A. 2019a. "Between freedom and regulation: Investigating community standards for enhancing scientific robustness of Citizen Science". In *Regulating new technologies in uncertain times*, ed. L. Reins, 31–46. Heidelberg: T.M.C. Asser Press, Springer-Verlag.

Berti Suman, A. 2019b. "The role of information in multilateral governance of environmental health risk: Lessons from the Equatorial Asian Haze case." *Journal of Risk Research* 25 (8),Special Issue on 'Multilateral Governance of Technological Risk'. https://doi.org/10.1080/13669877.2019.1617338.

Berti Suman, A. 2021. *The Policy Uptake of Citizen Sensing*. Cheltenham: Edward Elgar.

Berti Suman, A. 2023. "Citizen-gathered data to support public services under emergencies: Promises and perils of openness." *The Journal of Open Access to Law* 11 (2).

Berti Suman, A., and R. Pierce. 2018. "Challenges for citizen science and the EU Open Science agenda under the GDPR." *European Data Protection Law Review* 4 (3): 284–295. https://doi.org/10.21552/edpl/2018/3/7.

Berti Suman, A., S. Schade and Y. Abe. 2020. "Exploring legitimization strategies for contested uses of citizen-generated data for policy." *The Journal of Human Rights and the Environment* 11, Special issue: From Student Strikes to the Extinction Rebellion. https://doi.org/10.4337/9781800881099.

Bijker, W.E., R. Bal, and R. Hendriks. 2009. *The paradox of scientific authority: The role of scientific advice in democracies*. Cambridge, MA: The MIT Press.

Boholm, A., H. Corvellec, and M. Karlsson. 2012. "The practice of risk governance: Lessons from the field. *Journal of Risk Research* 15 (1): 1–20.

Boulos, K., B. Resch, D.N. Crowley, J.G. Breslin, G. Sohn, R. Burtner, W.A. Pike, et al. 2011. "Crowdsourcing, citizen sensing and sensor web technologies for public and environmental health surveillance and crisis management: Trends, OGC standards and application examples." *International Journal of Health Geographics* 10 (67): 67–96. https://doi.org/10.1186/1476-072X-10-67.

Brandsen, T., and M. Honingh. 2016. "Distinguishing different types of coproduction: A conceptual analysis based on the classical definitions." *Public Administration Review* 76: 427–435. https://doi.org/10.1111/puar.12465.

Castells, M. 1996. *The rise of the network society: The information age: economy, society, and culture*, vol. 1, no. 2. Malden, MA: Wiley-Blackwell.

Chilvers, J., and M. Kearnes. 2015. *Remaking participation: Science, environment and emergent publics*. London: Taylor and Francis.

Corburn, J. 2005. *Street science: Community knowledge and environmental health justice*. Cambridge, MA: The MIT Press.

Dewey, J. 1927. *The public and its problems*. Oxford, UK: Holt.

Douglas, H. 2009. *Science, policy, and the value-free ideal*. Pittsburg: University of Pittsburgh Press.

Ezrahi, Y. 1990. *The descent of Icarus: Science and the transformation of contemporary democracy*. Cambridge, MA: Harvard University Press.

Ezrahi. 2012. *Imagined democracies: Necessary political fictions*. New York: Cambridge University Press.

Figueiredo Nascimento, S., E. Cuccillato, S. Schade and A. Guimarães Pereira. 2016. *Citizen engagement in science and policy-making*. EUR 28328 EN. Luxembourg: Publications Office of the European Union.

Funtowicz, S.O., and J.R. Ravetz. 1993. "Science for the post-normal age." *Futures* 25 (7): 739–755.

Garrelts, H., and H. Lange. 2011. "Path dependencies and path change in complex fields of action: Climate adaptation policies in Germany in the realm of flood risk management." *Ambio* 40 (2): 200–209. https://doi.org/10.1007/s13280-010-0131-3.

Giddens, A. 1990. *The consequences of modernity*. Cambridge, UK: Polity Press.

Gieryn, T.F. 1983. "Boundary-work and the demarcation of science from non-science: Strains and interests in professional ideologies of scientists." *American Sociological Review* 48: 781–795.

Gieryn, T.F. 1999. *Cultural boundaries of science: Credibility on the line*. University of Chicago Press.

Habermas, J. 1991. *The structural transformation of the public sphere. An inquiry into a category of bourgeois society*, trans. T. Burger. Cambridge: The MIT Press.

Hicks, A., J. Barclay, J. Chilvers, M.T. Armijos, K. Oven, P. Simmons and M. Haklay. 2019. "Global Mapping of Citizen Science Projects for Disaster Risk Reduction." *Frontiers in Earth Science* 7(226). https://doi.org/10.3389/feart.2019.00226.

International Risk Governance Council - IRGC. 2005. *Risk Governance: Towards an Integrative Approach*. White Paper No. 1 by Renn, O., with Annex by Graham, P. Geneva: IRGC.

Irwin, A., T. Jensen, and K. Jones. 2013. "The good, the bad and the perfect: Criticizing engagement practice." *Social Studies of Science* 43: 118–135.

Jasanoff, S., ed. 2004. *States of knowledge: The co-production of science and social order*. Abingdon: Routledge.

Jasanoff, S. 2003. "Technologies of humility: Citizen participation in governing science." *Minerva* 41: 223–244.

Jasanoff, S. 2005. *Designs on nature: Science and democracy in Europe and the United States*. Princeton University Press.

Jasanoff, S., and S.H. Kim. 2013. "Sociotechnical imaginaries and national energy policies." *Science as Culture* 22 (2): 189–196. https://doi.org/10.1080/09505431.2013.786990.

Jasanoff, S.S. 1987. "Contested boundaries in policy-relevant science." *Social Studies of Science* 17 (2): 195–230.

Law, J. 2015. *STS as a method*. Department of Sociology, The Open University. http://heterogeneities.net/publications/Law2015STSAsMethod.pdf.

Luhmann, N. 1993. "Ecological communication: Coping with the unknown." *Systems Practice* 6 (5): 527–539. https://doi.org/10.1007/BF01059510.

Mahlouly, D. 2013. "Rethinking the public sphere in a digital environment: Similarities between the eighteenth and the twenty-first centuries." *Esharp* 20 (6): 1–21.

Ostrom, E. 1996. "Crossing the great divide: Coproduction, synergy, and development." *World Development* 24 (6): 1073–1087.

Paul, J.D., et al. 2018. "Citizen science for hydrological risk reduction and resilience building." *Wires Water* 5: 1. https://doi.org/10.1002/wat2.1262.

Power, M. 2007. *Organized uncertainty: Designing a world of risk management*. Oxford: Oxford University Press.

Renn, O., A. Klinke, and M. van Asselt. 2011. "Coping with complexity, uncertainty and ambiguity in risk governance: A synthesis." *Ambio* 40: 231–246. https://doi.org/10.1007/s13280-010-0134-0.

Rutz, S.I., S.A. Adams, S.E. Buitendijk, P.B.M. Robben, and A.A. de Bont. 2013. "Hiding complexity, uncertainty and ambiguity: How inspectorates simplify issues to create enforceable action." *Health, Risk & Society* 15 (4): 363–379. https://doi.org/10.1080/13698575.2013.796343.

Shackley, S., and B. Wynne. 1996. "Representing uncertainty in global climate change and policy: Boundary-ordering devices and authority." *Science, Technology, and Human Values* 21: 275–302.

Spruijt, P., A.B. Knol, E. Vasileiadou, J. Devilee, E. Lebret, and A.C. Petersen. 2014. "Roles of scientists as policy advisers on complex issues: A literature review." *Environmental Science & Policy* 40: 16–25. https://doi.org/10.1016/j.envsci.2014.03.002.

Star, S.L., and J.R. Griesemar. 1989. "Institutional ecology, 'translations', and boundary objects: Amateurs and professionals in Berkeley's Museum of Vertebrate Zoology, 1907–1939." *Social Studies of Science* 19: 387–420.

Teisman, G.R., and E.H. Klijn. 2008. "Complexity theory and public management." *Public Management Review* 10 (3): 287–297. https://doi.org/10.1080/14719030802002451.

Weingart, P. 1999. "Scientific expertise and political accountability: Paradoxes of science in politics." *Science and Public Policy* 26 (3): 151–161.

World Health Organization—WHO. 2013. *Health and environment: Communicating the risks*. Italy: Grafiche Antiga Spa.

Wynne, B. 1982. *Rationality and ritual: The windscale inquiry and nuclear decision making in Britain*. British Society for the History of Science.

Wynne, B. 1992. "Misunderstood misunderstanding: Social identities and public uptake of science." *Public Understanding of Science* 1 (3): 281–304. https://doi.org/10.1088/0963-6625/1/3/004.

Wynne, B. 1996. "May the sheep safely graze? A reflexive view of the expert-lay knowledge divide." In *Risk, environment and modernity*, ed. S. Lash, B. Szerszynski, and B. Wynne, 44–83. Los Angeles: Sage.

CHAPTER 5

Conclusion

Abstract This chapter develops conclusive reflections and builds a bridge to a future research agenda for researchers, interested civil society and practitioners. Discussing the main findings of the previous chapters, the conclusion posits that citizen sensing has the potential to contribute to the achievement of a more accountable and inclusive risk governance, especially in case of highly debated, ambiguous and politicized risks. This may improve risk governance by means of a twofold process, i.e., frictions with institutions in an early stage which may lead to convergence (that is, cooperation with the risk governors). It is argued that a clash of methods between the grassroots' and the institutional risk governance is regarded as constructive and positive. When a later convergence with the institutional system occurs ('policy uptake'), I argue that this outcome should be regarded as a success for the initiative and for the institution and a demonstration that the two approaches can strengthen and complement each other. However, context-dependency and other nuances are outlined as important factors to be considered.

Keywords Future research agenda · Conflict · Convergence · Policy uptake

A. Berti Suman, *Citizen Sensing for Risk Response*,
https://doi.org/10.1007/978-3-032-03939-2_5

Key Takeaways From the Study

Throughout the reflections developed in this book, I laid the theoretical foundations for the need to explore the potential contribution that citizen sensing can offer to (environmental) risk governance, starting from the perceived legitimacy gaps in current institutional approaches to governing risks. I developed a sociological argument that citizen sensing has the potential to respond to a legitimacy crisis in risk governance.

I answered the question on the gaps of the dominant models of environmental health risk governance, as perceived by lay citizens, through a tripartite approach. I started identifying and problematizing the definitions of the key elements of this research, i.e., public and environmental health; risk and environmental health risk; governance and risk governance. Second, I discussed and problematized the arguably 'dominant' models of environmental health risk governance. Lastly, based on these arguments, I sketched a 'theory of change' of risk governance based on citizen sensing to be explored through theoretical and empirical analyses in future research (as already done in the case studies analysed by Berti Suman et al. 2020 and Berti Suman 2021b) and across fields (from data visualization of risk, such as in Berti Suman 2020a; to innovation from below in risk governance, such as in Berti Suman 2020b; to urban health and multi-stakeholders' cooperation, such as in Berti Suman 2020c; to the sustainability nexus such as in Berti Suman et al. 2025 [Gharesifard, M., Ceccaroni, L., Gold, M., Berti Suman, A. and Das, K. (2025) "Citizen science and the nexus approach: unlocking synergies for sustainable development". Sustainability Nexus Forum, 33, 4.https://doi.org/10.1007/s00550-025-00562-4; to the legal sphere in terms of access to environmental information and the Aarhus Convention, such as in Berti Suman et al. 2023 [source: Berti Suman, A., Balestrini, M., Haklay, M. and Schade, S. (2023) "When Concerned People Produce Environmental Information: A Need to Re-Think Existing Legal Frameworks and Governance Models?" Citizen Science: Theory and Practice, 8(1).https://doi.org/10.5334/cstp.496 and in Berti Suman 2021a, and in terms of environmental law enforcement, such as in Berti Suman 2024). [source: Berti Suman A. (2024) "Civic Monitoring for Environmental Law Enforcement". Edward Elgar Publishing. ISBN: 978-1-0353-2869-7. http://www.e-elgar.com/shop/gbp/civic-monitoring-for-environmental-law-enforcement-9781035328697.html]

In light of the preceding discussion and of the three goals of this book, I can summarize the following findings:

- First, the current definitions of public health, environmental health, risk, risk governance, and environmental health risk governance are all but uncontested and are undergoing a process of re-definition performed by academics, institutions and civil society. The drafting of working definitions for each of these concepts seemed indispensable to proceed with the analysis. Summarizing here these working definitions, environmental health risk governance is understood both as the web of interactions between a multitude of actors and a framework for organizing and managing uncertain events (e.g., a radiation leak) or phenomena (e.g., noise) that are likely to affect public health, but there is scientific uncertainty or disagreement on whether the consequences of this event will be harmful for public health.
- Second, the discussed dominant models of environmental health risk governance present gaps and shortcomings which stimulated an inquiry on how (some of) these gaps may be tackled by citizen sensing. Citizen sensing under this perspective would derive from dissatisfaction and distrust towards the institutional system of risk governance and from the need to challenge informational monopolies and dogmatic ways of governing (or ignoring) the risk. This sense of distrust has been investigated in the book through empirical analyses.
- Third, there are theoretical foundations justifying an attempt to constructively integrate citizen sensing in the current models of risk governance. First, citizen sensing could have the potential to contribute to the achievement of a more accountable and more inclusive risk governance, especially in case of highly debated, ambiguous and politicized risks. Second, citizen sensing may overturn the assumed negative relationship between technology and environmental health. The book framed citizen sensing as an opportunity for society to use technology positively, to improve societal response to environmental challenges. Lastly, the inclusion of the knowledge stemming from citizen sensing practices to inform policy-making and regulations over risk problems could be useful for increasing the social legitimacy of such interventions.

Related to the last finding, it has been noted in this book that citizen sensing could improve risk governance by means of a twofold process, through possible frictions which can eventually lead to convergence. A clash of methods between the grassroots and the institutional risk governance is regarded as constructive and positive. When a later convergence with the institutional system occurs, I argued that this outcome should be regarded as a success for the initiative and for the institution (framed here as the 'policy uptake' of citizen sensing, or—in other words—its influence on and contribution to governing the risk) and a demonstration that the two approaches can strengthen and complement each other (Berti Suman 2018).

In spite of the conceivable benefits of citizen sensing, it is also true that the collection of 'alternative' and competing data could undermine the authority of the institutions democratically appointed as responsible for the risk problem. This reliance on conflicting data could cause more chaos than clarity and substantially delay the problem-solving process (Berti Suman 2018). The outlined conflicting scenario could be solved by including the citizens' input before the rise of the conflict (but, again, with mechanisms to prevent unfounded claims) in ordinary governance strategies, which could arguably mitigate the perceived need for evidence-checking ex-post.

Case Insight 4: Creating Spaces for Reactive Citizen Science

In this case insight, I connect the reflections developed in this book with some of the findings of the Marie Skłodowska-Curie Action-funded "Sensing for Justice" (SensJus) project.[1] SensJus researched the potential of grassroots-driven environmental (health) monitoring, i.e., reactive citizen science, as a source of evidence in environmental justice litigation (starting from the U.S.-based Formosa Plastics case, Berti Suman and Schade 2021), and as a tool for conflict mediation in extra-judicial setting. The research focused not only on environmental risk management experts and citizen science communities, but also on practitioners

[1] Marie Skłodowska-Curie Individual Fellowship, grant n. 891513 (2021–2023), awarded to author Anna Berti Suman under H2020-EU. Pilot research for the SensJus project has been supported by the Dutch Research Council Rubicon Fellowship n. 019.193SG.007 (2020–2021). See https://sensingforjustice.webnode.it/ and https://joint-research-centre.ec.europa.eu/projects-and-activities/innovations-public-governance/civic-monitoring-environmental-enforcement_en.

in the field of environmental and climate justice (e.g., lawyers and judges engaged in strategic litigation). Therefore, this book was shaped in a way that can be of help also of these publics.

The SensJus project targeted especially grey zones of citizen science and sensing where its recognition and valorization are more difficult than for established, larger-scale, institutionally funded initiatives. The project observed in particular very local, spontaneous, small-scale and low-budget initiatives that are not supported by a public agency nor linked with an academic institution and that deploy in contexts dominated by high social distrust and conflict. SensJus explored through fieldwork specific instances of this type of citizen science, for example, in Basilicata where lay people are monitoring the impact of oil pollution on their land, exposing themselves to legal risks and to risks for their own health. SensJus also analysed less conventional forms of citizen science and citizen sensing such as how to valorise the evidence gathered from communities affected by the impacts of climate change, including those people forced to migrate due to an extreme climate event (e.g., Berti Suman and Burnette 2024). The key aim of the inquiry was to promote policy, legal and judicial uptake of these forms of citizen science, as discussed in the final book stemming from the project titled "Civic Monitoring for Environmental Law Enforcement" (Berti Suman 2024).

The findings originated from SensJus inquiry resonates with some of the arguments advanced in this book as they suggest the need to establish spaces, which can be legal clinics at universities, museums, libraries or other public spaces where ordinary people, experts and students can cooperate to advise grassroots citizen sensing initiatives and assure them support in order to comply with applicable laws and regulations. These clinics—taking inspiration from U.S. experiences[2]—could also provide support to avoid liabilities and health risks for participants stemming from citizen science. Lastly, these spaces could provide support to citizen science communities in terms of data management in the short and long term.

This empirical and theoretical inquiry also urges the recognition at a legal (as suggested and concretely outlined in Berti Suman 2021a) or at least political level of more 'reactive' forms of citizen science such as the

[2] See https://citizenscience.org/get-involved/working-groups/law-policy/ask-a-legal-question/.

AnalyzeBasilicata campaign in Italy[3] that are struggling to get funding and visibility, yet offering a precious service of environmental information dissemination (Berti Suman 2022). Academics and professionals in the field should engage in a discussion on how to support these civic sentinels through creative forms, for example, through the establishment of labour unions dedicated to citizen scientists.

SensJus also explored creative forms of communication that bring a wider audience closer to civic monitoring, for example, through drawings and story-telling. For example, the project produced a graphic novel (Berti Suman et al. 2021) in open access in four languages (Italian, English, Spanish and French) recounting the story of a civic sentinel facing oil contamination in an imaginary land.[4] Furthermore, the project engaged in creating a theatre performance based on the experience of local inhabitants in relation to oil extraction.[5] This method of communication facilitated a dialogue also with low literacy participants such as those encountered during the fieldwork. The discussion developed in this book and specifically in this case box will hopefully inspire a work of drafting a 'manifesto' to ensure that reactive environmental citizen science can flourish and increase its impact, both from the perspective of substantial and methodological approaches.

Limitations of the Study

As a concluding remark, I wish to stress that the successful integration of citizen sensing in institutional risk governance has been discussed here in general and in situated instances. However, citizen sensing practices are highly dependent on the context of reference, and no universal answer can be given to the question: "Can citizen sensing contribute to risk governance?" The context-dependency of citizen sensing seems to suggest that a deep scrutiny of the empirical reality of the practice is necessary. Only from the analysis of a relatively large and representative number of case studies, it is possible reach generalizable conclusions yet bearing in mind that the policy uptake of citizen sensing may depend on changing, context-related factors that cannot be captured in the present analysis.

[3] See https://covacontro.org/.

[4] See https://sensingforjustice.webnode.it/l/fumetto/.

[5] See https://www.youtube.com/watch?v=zjUt2qsswlA (minute 35:35).

In addition, the notions discussed in Chapter 2 such as environmental health and public health are all but universal. In fact, they are shaped by values and identities of specific communities where these concepts are performed or manifest, as recently discussed by JRC scientists in a policy-maker's guide (Scharfbillig et al. 2021). Furthermore, this book focused on theories and cases that stress the crisis of legitimacy towards science and towards official risk governance. The COVID-19 pandemic showed the need to rely on sound science, verified data infrastructures and safe communication channels. It pushed larger sectors of society to regain high trust in science but also augmented or generated the scepticism of others towards science, in particular around vaccines. At present, geopolitical tensions including the multiplication of armed conflicts and an increasing security discourse is undermining again trust in science and in public participation, but this could be the object of another book.

In addition, the book focused mostly on risk, environmental risk and governance *in relation to* citizen sensing and thus did not engage critically with equal depth with the notion of citizen sensing, unpacked in my book "The Policy Uptake of Citizen Sensing"—"Chapter 2: Setting the scene: what is citizen sensing?" (Berti Suman 2021b). That chapter also outlines the limitations of the practice, including inequalities that persist despite multiple engagement efforts, and its promises in terms of socio-technical and even policy and legislative and policy advancements. Counter-measures to the outlined weaknesses of citizen sensing discussed in the book are flanked with another book providing an accessible 'toolbox' for interested communities, policy-makers and researchers that wish citizen sensing to structurally contribute to risk governance (Berti Suman 2020d).

Also worth mentioning are the time and geographical limitations of the study on which this book is built. The data collection for this study concluded in summer 2022 and focused on selected empirical cases. At the time of reviewing this study, in summer 2025, the current geopolitical situation affecting world society poses new challenges for the environment and new scenarios and places for the engagement of citizen sensing practices. A (relatively new) front for these initiatives is manifesting the mapping and reporting of environmental harms associated with armed conflicts. A project in which I personally contributed from the angle of civic environmental monitoring is the "Gromada" project aimed at developing cooperation between European universities to support public and legal capacity for environmental recovery in war-torn Ukraine. Starting from the impacts of the Russian full-scale invasion on Ukraine's environment, the project explores and supports civic engagement practices in environmental monitoring by analysing barriers and opportunities for the practice and its deployment for justice and peacebuilding.[6]

References

Berti Suman, A. 2018. "Challenging risk governance patterns through citizen sensing: The Schiphol Airport case." *International Review of Law, Computers & Technology* 32 (1). https://doi.org/10.1080/13600869.2018.1429186.

Berti Suman, A. 2020a. "Making visible politically masked risks: The haze case of bottom-up data visualization." In *Data visualization in society*, ed. H. Kennedy and M. Engebretsen, 425–440. Amsterdam: Amsterdam University Press.

Berti Suman, A. 2020b. "Innovating societal response to radiation risk: Insights from the Fukushima Safecast case." *The IUCN Academy of Environmental Law Series*. Cheltenham: Edward Elgar.

Berti Suman, A. 2020c. "Multi-stakeholder cooperation for safe and healthy urban environments: The case of citizen sensing." In *Partnerships for livable cities*, ed. C. van Montfort and A. Michels. London: Palgrave.

Berti Suman, A. 2020d. *Sensing the risk. A case for integrating citizen sensing into risk governance*. Tilburg: Open Press Tilburg University.

Berti Suman, A. 2021a. "Citizen sensing from a legal standpoint: Legitimizing the practice under the Aarhus framework." *The Journal for European Environmental & Planning Law*. https://doi.org/10.1163/18760104-18010003

Berti Suman, A. 2021b. *The policy uptake of citizen sensing*. Cheltenham: Edward Elgar.

Berti Suman, A. 2024. *Civic monitoring for environmental law enforcement*. Cheltenham: Edward Elgar.

Berti Suman, A. and S. Schade. 2021. "The Formosa case: A step forward on the acceptance of citizen-collected evidence in environmental litigation?" *Citizen Science: Theory and Practice* 6 (1): 16, 1–13. https://doi.org/10.5334/cstp.367.

[6] Inspired by this project, in 2025 I co-founded a new Working Group of the European Citizen Science Association (ECSA) to fuel a broader discussion on citizen science in areas affected by armed conflicts, which is gaining considerable interest from the scientific community and from civil society. The Gromada Erasmus KA2 + project, grant n. 2023-1-SE01-KA220-HED-000151848 (2023-2025). See https://gromada-erasmus.eu/.

Berti Suman, A. and A. Burnette. 2024. "A place for people's knowledge in climate evidence: Exploring civic evidence in climate litigation." *Review of European, Comparative & International Environmental Law* 33 (3). https://doi.org/10.1111/reel.12552.

Berti Suman, A., A. Toietta and S. Schade. 2021. *Story of a civic sentinel.* A graphic novel produced by the SensJus project and printed by the European Commission's JRC. https://sensingforjustice.webnode.it/l/fumetto/.

Berti Suman, A. 2022. "Striving for good environmental information: Civic sentinels of oil pollution in the south of the north." *Law, Environment and Development Journal* 17.

Berti Suman, A., S. Schade and Y. Abe. 2020. "Exploring legitimization strategies for contested uses of citizen-generated data for policy." *The Journal of Human Rights and the Environment* 11, Special issue: From Student Strikes to the Extinction Rebellion. https://doi.org/10.4337/97818008810.

Scharfbillig, M., et al. 2021. *Values and Identities—A policymaker's guide.* Luxembourg: Publications Office of the European Union. https://doi.org/10.2760/349527.

Index

C
citizen sensing, vii, viii, 1–4, 8–11, 16, 21–23, 25–27, 29, 36, 39–44, 58, 59, 63, 65, 68, 69, 72, 74, 75, 77, 83, 86–90, 93, 95–99, 101, 102, 104–107, 116–121
conflict, viii, 36, 40, 70, 71, 86, 96, 101, 102, 118, 119
convergence, viii, 118
crisis, 2, 87, 102, 116, 121

D
data infrastructures, vii, 121
distrust, vii, viii, 3, 37, 73, 103, 117, 119

E
environmental health, 2, 3, 8, 12–14, 16–18, 20–22, 42, 46, 57, 69, 72, 73, 89, 94, 106, 116, 117, 121
expert interviews, 62, 82, 83, 85, 95–98
expertise, 25, 60, 82, 86, 100, 101

F
future research agenda, 116

G
governance innovation, 116

I
informational gaps, vii

L
lay knowledge, 2, 25, 37, 59, 64, 82–86, 99, 103
legitimacy, vii, 1, 8, 11, 13, 23, 45, 59, 69–71, 86–88, 99, 101, 102, 104, 105, 116, 117, 121

M
mixed-methods approach, viii

P
policy uptake, viii, 2, 25, 39, 82, 97, 98, 118, 120

A. Berti Suman, *Citizen Sensing for Risk Response*,
https://doi.org/10.1007/978-3-032-03939-2

public health, vii, 2, 3, 8–13, 18, 20–22, 31, 41, 42, 45, 67, 68, 70, 73, 82, 94, 100, 117, 121
public participation, 73

R
reference notions, 2
risk governance, vii, viii, 1–3, 8, 9, 22, 23, 25, 28, 29, 32, 36–40, 42, 44–47, 57–61, 63–71, 73–77, 82, 87–90, 93–101, 104–108, 116–118, 120, 121
risk governance models, 89, 95

S
sensor technology, vii

T
theory of change, 2, 3, 82, 89, 116

Kolibri 360 GmbH
Ferdinand-Jühlke-Straße 7
99095 Erfurt, Deutschland
produktsicherheit@kolibri360.de